WHO'S

YOUR

DADDY?

By

Ray Mingo

WHO'S YOUR DADDY?

Copyright © 2020 by Ray Mingo.

PUBLISHER'S NOTE:

This book does not claim to be the "bible" on the topic of fatherhood, but is written to express the author's views and personal research on some of the core issues pertaining to non-residential fathers.

TABLE OF CONTENTS

FOREWORD

We have been invited to read a book, digest its content and work out its truths. Men, our children depend on us doing just that. In this book, the author tells us in so many words that he doesn't want to be preachy, nor do I. But read the statistics that he gives us. Read the suggestions and advice he puts before us. Fathers, let's *become* FATHERS.

PROTECTION

There was a time in history when the fathers and men in a village watched over the communities at night. Their communities had no walls, moats, armies or law enforcement to keep them safe. Most of those villages were in the deserts, mountains, plains or jungles and were vulnerable to natural predators and occurrences. Nocturnal predators waited for the cover of night to kill and eat easy prey.

The thieves of those days were somewhat like the "wolf packs" we had in Philly at one time. A gang of youth would go to a part of the city where people (many of whom were guests to the city) gathered for entertainment for an evening or weekend. Not thinking of danger or prepared to defend themselves, they were at the mercy of a horde of ten to twenty young men intent on mugging them. These young men ran through the unsuspecting mass of partyers, punching them and beating them with whatever they had on hand, robbing them. The whole thing was over in a couple of minutes.

Men and fathers centuries ago would guard their communities against gangs who came on foot, horseback or camel. In those times, the invaders would attempt to kill and kidnap the most vulnerable and take everything of value. Fathers, our children are similar to those most vulnerable in the town that have no protection.

PROVISION

Centuries ago, and even today in this society, individual fathers or fathers as a group would go hunting, fishing and gathering plants, giving food for their community/family. You will find the author telling us that our children need us to be involved providers. Mothers, grandparents and others can give in our absence, but there is still the emotional and spiritual support left that only a dad can give.

INSTRUCTION

Thousands of years ago when their sons reached a certain age, fathers would begin to teach their sons at home and in the village such things as the art of self-defense, hunting, gathering and fishing. These fathers sat with their boys to teach them through storytelling their family history and heritage. In many Jewish homes today, at the age of thirteen, a boy becomes a man and is seen differently, purposely prepared for his future. In like manner, in many Latino families, a young girl at the age of fifteen experiences her quinceanera and is then treated as a young woman. Dads, our children need our godly teaching.

The author of this book is reminding us that we have the same responsibilities, not just to our sons, but to our daughters as well. Protecting, providing and giving instruction (word and action) is a powerful and wonderful privilege and responsibility. We are fathers, we are parents, and we nurture and protect our offspring. We are those who help our children to be who they are. We caused them to come into being, brought them into existence and contributed to procreate and father them. Men, let's parent them. We caused them to be; now let's cause them to *become*.

LOST OPPORTUNITIES

Ray (the author) and I have participated in each other's lives for about forty years. We met during his early teen years and grew together emotionally and spiritually over the years. My wife and I became family with his wife and children. In all the good, bad, fun, confusing and mind-numbing times, he did not forget "fatherhood." He strove to keep a strong relationship with his daughters and raise three of them together, even though they have different mothers.

Out of those same good, tough, fun, confusing and mind-numbing times, Ray writes this book. This book has the potential to provoke thought and enlighten, challenge and inspire readers. Not every line might leave the reader in a *feel-good* place, but it will cause profound thought about its message. And when the reader is ready to grow, he will receive that message.

REDEEMING RELATIONSHIPS

In this book, Ray also talks about opportunities lost. There was a preacher and apostle in the Holy Scriptures who said: "Redeem the time because the days are evil." (Ephesians 5:16) That preacher and apostle, Paul, asks us to live our lives carefully, not as fools, but as those who are wisely utilizing the time at hand.

Fathers, we can all restart and move forward. Trying to revive relationships might not look the way we've imagined. It may even be difficult at times, but be encouraged! Bravely push *restart* and see what gifts might lie ahead as you faithfully pursue FATHERHOOD.

-   *Dr. Floyd R. Wheeler, Sr.*

Husband, Dad, Pastor, Mentor- Ray's Friend

ACKNOWLEDGMENTS

Roland Warren and National Fatherhood Initiative

SKIP and Mrs. Gloria Jean Canty-Williams

Dr. Ken R. Canfield of National Center for Fathering and National Responsible Fatherhood Clearinghouse

SingleFathers.org

Wallace McLaughlin, Ph.D., President/CEO of Fathers and Family
Center

Rachel Slaughter, M.Ed., Executive Director of The Salt and Light Learning Institute

GLENN SACKS of Fathers & Families

North Carolina Cooperative Extension

And special loving thanks to my mom Rosalee Mingo for being my mom. My sister Valerie and brother Rodney for being there for me in my time of need. And my dad for his courageous attempt at fatherhood.

And to Pastor Floyd Wheeler for taking me in and giving me my foundation of fatherhood with his lovely wife, Nancy Wheeler.

And to my three beautiful, bright and gifted daughters: Brittany, Ashley and Gianna; you all have made me proud to be called your Daddy. Love you girls!

INTRODUCTION

There is a cause that has the power to change the course of society, heal the ills of our communities and determine the future of our very existence. It is a cause of great significance, but the importance of its relevance has been weakened by the prison system, capitalism, social genocide, irresponsibility and absenteeism. Yet the power of this cause remains unmatched, unmistakable and irreplaceable with the positive effects of this cause on society being absolute and irrefutable. With that being said, I am honored and grateful to share my thoughts on this most important cause. We who call ourselves men must recommit and realign ourselves to this endeavor, for it is the only real answer to some specific societal illnesses. That cause is fatherhood, and its effect is life-saving.

This book is written practically for those fathers who do not live under the same roof under which their children live. We know them as non-residential fathers, a group with which I identify. I am not an expert with one or multiple degree abbreviations following my name. I am not a social worker, family psychologist, nor do I work for family services. But I have an accumulation of over 18 years of experience in this most rewarding position that any person will ever hold (next to motherhood); that position is fatherhood. I have obtained three certifications that certifies me as a father; they are the birth certificates of my three daughters. Parenting is probably the only profession that certifies you before you graduate from the training for that *profession*, that is if you receive any training. One can never get prepared for parenthood, so it is up to every man and woman to prove that they're worthy of those certificates. This certificate is not a certificate of completion per se, but one that is deemed completed only by daily living up to the task of parenting.

My 18 years of experience consist of victories and defeats, tears of joy and tears of sadness, successes and failures and plenty of mistakes. But fatherhood remained my strongest passion in life and, no doubt, the desire of many other non-residential fathers. Even with the desire to be a good father, I struggled with feelings of insecurity and the fear of being a failure. These experiences, coupled with the love that I have for my daughters, are what motivated me to write this book. The non-residential fathers whom are involved in their children's lives are very seldom recognized or given credit like the fathers who are one-half of a two-parent household. Some fathers genuinely want to participate in their children's lives, but have allowed life circumstances to be an excuse for keeping them from this rewarding call; they have traded in greatness for mediocrity.

The most disparaging situation is that there are those fathers who want no involvement whatsoever in the lives of the children that they helped bring into this world. My only words to those fathers are that it's their loss! Unfortunately, it may be the loss of an unfortunate child or children who will suffer from the effects of an absent father. These scenarios are ultimately becoming part of a devastating staggering statistic.

I wrote this book to encourage all non-residential fathers who, despite adversities and circumstances, have remained faithful to the call of fatherhood. I praise you; I encourage you not to give up, not to give in and not to give away that which will be your children's your children's children 's legacy for ages to come.

I also want to appeal to the hearts of fathers who are not involved in their children's life, to start. To urge them to get involved because their kids need their involvement. Not only do they need it, but they want it. They need your nurturing and crave your love. They want and need to hear from you. With the eyes of wandering souls, they are looking for your guidance. They are you, and you are them.

Fathers are like watchmen who stand on the walls of life, watching over and protecting their children from those who seek to invade and harm them. We must be diligent sentinels, for we are the protectors of our seed and the preservers of our posterity. We are the keepers of life's most precious and natural resources: our sons and daughters. We are the homeland security for our children. There is no greater cause for which a man should sacrifice himself, and there is no higher duty he will ever perform than that of being a father.

Fathers are so important that even God Himself chooses to reveal Himself as a Father and regards those He created as His children. There is very little difference in the attributes and characteristics of God and that of a father. These attributes are unchanging, unbreakable, uncompromising and unmistakable, with effects that are life-changing and life-saving. They bring along with them, judgment and mercy. They are loving, patient and nurturing, and most of all, they are involved. Without a father's presence, some unfortunate child would be doomed to walk in darkness.

This book is not written to discuss the problems that caused your failed marriage/relationship, nor is it to discuss how to repair it. The Bible never indicates that the Samaritan woman at the wheel became a believer, nor did it give any indication that her marriage situation was fixed. Her testimony was not so much of what Jesus did *for* her life, but of what he knew *about* her life. But yet her testimony of Jesus recognizing her plight without ever changing it, was enough to cause many others to believe.

God doesn't necessarily have to change your circumstances to use and do something great in your life, even as unfortunate as a divorce or separation may be. The state of your affairs neither disqualifies nor relieves you as men from the responsibility of fatherhood, and is not central to the context of this book. We should never divorce ourselves from our children. Precious time should not be wasted feuding and blaming each other, whether justifiable or unjustifiable; what's has been done is done. It should not prevent us from fulfilling our duty as fathers, as parents. We should love our children and be an intricate part of their lives despite the circumstance of divorce. There is only one way to answer this call to duty (fatherhood) and to carry out its mission, and that is through active unconditional loving, being involved in the lives of our children. The purpose is to be a father to those who did not ask to be born into this world. This mission should not be aborted for any reason. Failing this mission is unacceptable and unconscionable for any man.

We spend too much time fighting the war between spouses or exes, while our children become casualties of this relentless war. We spend too much time pointing the fingers at who is to blame for the breakup of our relationships, when we should be actively involved with our children, loving and pointing them in the right direction. Parents are fighting and feuding, flipping in and out of family court, trying to get the upper hand on each other, unconsciously destroying the very two people a child needs. This kind of judicial gymnastics only serves the selfish interest of the parents and not the best interest of their children. Eventually it becomes more about two parents trying to get back at one another. It's become a vindictive battle based on money. Fathers determine that "she's not going to get my money" and mothers vow, "I'm going to take him for everything he's worth; this will teach him." When we as parents engage in such behaviors, this is not indicative of what's best for the child, but what's best for the parents. With plenty of money in both parents' pockets, they leave behind children who are in an emotional, mental and spiritual deficit. You will find no tossing blame around in this book, only a guide to the pursuit of fatherhood.

What doctor would be a good doctor if he sat at the bedside of his sick patient blaming him for the poor choices he's made in his life that brought him to that sickly state? A good doctor would do everything in his power to make sure that the person gets well; he would recommend lifestyle changes needed to avoid any future problems. Just as a good doctor, you can expect the same advice from me throughout this book. No blame, no judgment, no running people down, only encouragement and a look at what could happen if we give up the pursuit of fatherhood. Who's at fault? That's irrelevant. The kind of father that we should be is relevant.

Chapter 1:

I REMEMBER THE TIMES

Words cannot begin to express just how much a child can gain from having a non-residential father involved in his or her life. Fatherhood begins at pregnancy, following birth into the teen years of a child, and is crucial throughout the mistakes and curiosities of adolescence into the choices of adulthood. Lost time can never be regained; memories of what could have been, can't be magically produced. These memories can span from before they could speak to the time it was impossible to stop them from talking. Memories of when they relied on their father for everything to when their dependency upon you fades through the years. Memories of sadness and laughter, memories of failures and victories, memories of the best of times and the worst of times. Not only do these memories enrich our lives, but they allow us to create and strengthen a bond with our children. They will enable the father and child to grow together as one.

Every shared experience is another learning opportunity and serves as another building block on which to formulate the non-residential father and child relationship. It is only through active involvement in the lives of our children that we can create these priceless memories.

When my first marriage with the mother of my first and second daughters ended, I had no place to go. Thankfully, my brother, who owned a triplex, allowed me to live in one of the units. It was a basement that had a stove and a small bathroom with a shower. Despite my offering to pay for my stay, he would not accept any money for rent. I remember him telling me that I could stay there as long as it took for me to get myself together and that I should use the money to take care of my little girls. I don't know where I would have been if it were not for his generosity at that time in my life. The place was too small for me to have two little girls sleeping over for a weekend. Instead, I would pick them up, and we would go on frequent outings. It got to be very expensive at times, but was worth every dollar.

Then there was my other committed relationship, which produced my youngest daughter. This relationship ended after nine years. When it ended, I was fortunate to have been able to stay with my sister. She offered to let me stay with her until I could get back on my feet. Without any hesitation, she opened her doors to me and allowed me to stay in her relatively large one-bedroom apartment. I was grateful that she was there for me in those difficult times. Not only was my sister gracious enough to let me stay with her, but she allowed me to bring my kids over to visit every other weekend. She did this because she knew how much I loved my girls. She made this sacrifice for my children and me, even though it inconvenienced her. I will never forget her sacrifice of love.

I slept on a sofa bed when alone, and on the floor, the weekends that I had my daughters. The youngest daughters slept on the sofa bed. The oldest slept on the floor in the next room or with my sister in her room. My sister was going to make extensive renovations to accommodate my girls so that it would be comfortable for them. But, because of the financial cost of such improvements, I could not allow her to do that. So, we made the best of our situation. Ultimately, I was just so happy to have my girls that my circumstances did not matter.

Most nights, when I knew they were asleep, I laid there crying, feeling embarrassed, angry, sad and inadequate as a father. Depressed and downhearted, with tears streaming from my eyes, I could only pray and seek guidance from God. I felt that they deserved better from me; I felt like the one in whom they put their trust had let them down. I wondered what they thought of me as their father. But despite those thoughts and feelings, I was happy because they were there with me and they were together.

It was very crowded in that one-bedroom apartment on those weekends. My sister helped out in many ways, even to the extent of spending her money and doing things she did not have to do. I wanted my daughters with me so bad that I didn't think of how awkward and uncomfortable those crowded weekends were for them. Once I realized this, I had to make a decision that I didn't want to make. I explained to my daughters that I was no longer going to keep them overnight on our weekends together; this would be just until I could get my own place. In the meantime, I would pick them up every day on that weekend, and each day, we would do something fun or interesting. Afterward, I would take them to their homes so that they could sleep comfortably in their beds. I also informed my sister about my decision. She immediately began to come up with possible ideas that might convince me to do otherwise. I knew she was serious about these ideas, but I could no longer allow her to inconvenience herself because of the love and concern she had for me and her nieces. I knew my girls were uncomfortable but too afraid to tell me for fear that I would be hurt.

Every time I took them back to their homes, I worried about them. I felt I was their sole protector. If something were to happen to them, I would feel responsible because I was not there to protect them. These feelings were no reflection on the mothers of my children, because both were and are excellent and dedicated mothers. But I always felt that as a father, the protection and safety of my girls belonged exclusively to me.

Sometimes I felt overwhelming guilt because I could not physically be there with my three girls. The feeling of inadequacy was my burden to bear. But I knew of a Father, who is always present and all-knowing, a heavenly Father. In my time of trouble, I cried to Him, and He helped me. He is the Almighty God. He could be where I couldn't be. He could see what I could not see; His arms could reach where mine could not. So, I asked God to be a father to my girls. He made up for my limitations and frailties. God and I had shared custody of my children, me doing what I should do as a father, and Him doing what I couldn't do.

I was so determined to be a father to those girls who I helped bring into this world; I was willing to sacrifice my very life for them. Even though I made mistakes along the way, through it all, I was determined that I was going to be a presence in my daughters' lives, despite those mistakes.

Chapter 2:

WHO'S YOUR DADDY?

A man was walking down a country roadside when he noticed a boy doing something that he was not supposed to be doing. So, the man asked the child, "Boy, who's your daddy?" The boy replied, "I don't know; you have any ID?"

Fathers are like Easter eggs; they look different on the outside, but they are the same on the inside. Some fathers are like eggs in an Easter egg hunt; some are hard to find, some are not so hard to find and some never found. I want to purpose a question to all non-residential fathers: Who is your daddy? The answer to this question might be different for each father, not only because we have different fathers, but because we have had different experiences with our fathers, good and some bad. And in the cases where our experiences are similar, we have responded differently to them.

It is our experience and response to these experiences that have moulded us into the men we are today. Your experiences and responses can be the empowering factor contributing to you being the best non-residential or at-home father you can be. Or it could be the discouraging factor. The experiences of our fathers, how we responded to them and their interaction or non-interaction with us will be evident within us, setting a precedent for how we involve ourselves with our children. Interactions and non-interactions are responses to our experiences that are contagious and will spread to generations to come. They will spread to our children and have a profound impact on their well-being and what they do as parents.

As parents, we have been moulded partly by the type of relationship we have had with our parents, and by the kind of relationship we didn't have with them. That's why we must break any current molds that would negatively affect our children's future.

So, who's your daddy? What kind of interaction did you and him have with one another? Or was there any interaction at all? Have you ever seen your daddy? What kind of person was or is your daddy? Did your daddy live prudently in your presence, or did he live a reckless lifestyle before your very eyes? Did he live for the now, having no concern about his careless actions and lifestyle and the consequences those actions and lifestyle would have on you? Did he live in a way in which you could see that he cared for and loved you?

What type of relationship did your father have with your mother? Did your daddy play games with you? Did he share times of laughter and of sorrow with you? Was it a joy for you to see him when he came to visit you? Has he ever told you that he loved you? What was it, or is it about him that influenced you to become the father you are today?

It doesn't matter whether his influence was negative or positive, or whether or not he was there. It doesn't even matter about the answers you have to these questions. What does matter is how you have allowed it to affect you and how you respond to those experiences. Whatever the influence, be it bad or good, know that it takes the good as well as the bad to create something better.

Chapter 3:

IT'S ALL ABOUT THE B.A.G. LADIES

I have been so blessed with three beautiful girls, whom I call my B.A.G. LADIES; 'B' stands for Brittany, my firstborn, 'A' for Ashley, my next born or middle child, and 'G' for Gianna, my youngest. I cut the umbilical cord when Brittany and Ashley were born. Gianna was an emergency C-section preemie. I was living with my significant other at the time of her birth. After coming home from work, I felt a sense of emptiness, as though someone was missing. These feelings moved me to ask my significant other, who was pregnant with Gianna, how long was it since she felt the baby move in her stomach. She said, "A few days ago." She was convinced that it was normal, but for some strange reason, I was not so convinced. Still, with this feeling that someone was missing, I started nagging her to go to the hospital. At first, she refused. She said no several times, but because of my persistence, she soon gave in and agreed to go to the hospital.

To make a long story short, when we got to the hospital, the doctor said that if I hadn't been so persistent and if we'd waited a few minutes longer, Gianna would not be here. The nurse's words were that I saved her life. I say she is my life, as are my other two daughters. Their breath of life breathed life into me. They became my sole reason for living.

As I've mentioned earlier, two of my daughters share the same mother. My third daughter has a different mother. I've been in two committed relationships, totalling 20 something years between the two. This book is not to bash the women with whom I once had relationships or the women who gave birth to these precious girls of mine. It isn't about the things that went wrong in those two relationships. It isn't about blowing my own horn, writing about how good of a father I think I am. Lord knows I've made my share of mistakes as a father and as a husband. This book is not about my legal rights as the father of my children. This book is not about child support or visitation rights. I don't believe in that thing we call "legal rights" when it comes to being a parent.

I believe every parent has the God-given natural right and responsibility to be parents. Even animals know who their children are and take on the fundamental responsibility as parents, each playing their natural role. The purpose of this book is about being an involved, loving non-residential father to children that share our same genetics and has our blood running through their veins. It is about their God-given natural right to have a relationship with the man they call *daddy*, and about our responsibility as men not to take that right from them. For me, this book is and forever will be about my B.A.G. ladies.

Two factors motivated me to be actively involved in my children's life. One is obvious: I love those girls with everything that is in me. The other thing is, I've always said as a young man that if I ever had children, that I would never abandon them like my father abandoned my siblings and me; even though years after leaving us, he had a change of heart but died before that change could ever manifest itself. His change of heart killed him.

My motivation was my mother, who despite many external and internal obstacles and afflictions, never abandoned us. My life was always going to be about the B.A.G. ladies. I was never going to abandon them.

Chapter 4:

MY MOM

I remember growing up in the North Philly section of the city, and later on the East side Germantown section of Philadelphia. It was my sister Valerie, my brother Rodney, and I, raised by our wonderful mother, Rosalee Mingo. My mom was the only parent that I knew. Although not perfect, our mom raised us without the presence of a father. When times were hard, she never considered giving up or giving us up. She strived to make holidays special for us, even though she had a minimal income. She made sure we graduated from grade school, even though my brother and I managed to skip school quite a few times. We took advantage of the fact that she had to work many hours. Because of that, she could not keep track of us all the time.

My mom worked many hours for little money. We watched our mother struggle with the demons inside her, sometimes winning and sometimes losing the mental and emotional battles, but never surrendering to defeat; she knew she had the responsibility to raise three children. The woman we loved was plagued with deep emotional, mental and some may say, spiritual problems. The problems plagued her and were brought on by a series of nervous breakdowns, caused by an abusive alcoholic husband. These events happened long before I was old enough to remember.

Fortunately for us, she did not let her demons prevent her from being a mother. She was determined not to let her tragedies and circumstances prevent her from raising her children. In those days, my mom struggled with alcohol and was plagued by schizophrenia. Alcohol became her way to mask the pain of past hurts, and the only way that she could chase the demons of schizophrenia away. It became her way of healing a broken heart and helped suppress the bad memories. She eventually escaped the grips of alcohol through her self-will. But she could not escape the much tighter vice-like grips that depression and schizophrenia had on her.

There were times when we could hear our mother talking to herself as though other people were in the room with her, but there was no one there. But she had an uncanny ability to snap out of it when it came time to fulfil her motherly obligations. It was as though motherhood possessed her soul and kept her sane. It was evident; the demons she battled had to take a backseat to motherhood.

With all that you've read about our mother and us, I don't want you to think that our lives were just filled with tragedies. Yes, we had many adversities, but that's a story for another book. Amidst the many difficulties, there were good times, fun times, but most of all, in those times, we had each other. And through all these problems, my mother never abandoned us. She held on to just enough of her sanity so that she could raise us. She was determined to fulfil her motherly obligations through any means necessary; abandonment was never a choice.

This book is not written for or about mothers, but it was through a mother that I've learned what it meant to be a dedicated parent. It was through a mother that I got a glimpse of what fatherhood looked like, and it was through my mom that I've learned to respect the power of love.

The power of love transcends disabilities. It rises above our selfish needs to meet the needs of others. Despite one's personal shortcomings, faults and inabilities, love only seeks to serve the needs of others. No matter how low life brings you, a mother's love will pick you up. The power of a mother's love will be there. It will never abandon you. It is selfless. It is sacrificing, and most of all, it is authentic.

Chapter 5:
MY FATHER

"So many questions I must ask myself today...
What will I leave behind when life has passed my way?
Will people remember my name or forget me just the same?
Will I leave a trace of Jesus somewhere?
Have I been a light in dark places?
Brought a smile to sad faces?
Have I showed the world that I really care?
Have I lived my life the way He wants me to each and every day?
When someone stumbled was I there?
So many questions I must ask myself today...
What will I leave behind when life has passed my way?"

- *Lyrics from MANY QUESTIONS,*
Larnelle Harris, gospel singer/songwriter

It behoves us to take a minute and think about what we will leave behind after we've passed on. What impressions will we leave our children? What kind of children will we leave behind in the world, and what contribution will they have to give to the world?

The kind seeds you have sowed in your kids will determine the kind of impact that they will have on our future society. As alluded earlier, what we do with our children or what we don't do with them will impact them mentally, emotionally and spiritually, and how it impacts them is the kind of influence they will have. When I reminisce about my father, my only recollection is of two events in my life that I could remember seeing him. These two times stuck out to me like a fox in a hen house. Those times were probably just as devouring to my emotional, mental and spiritual being as that fox was to those hens.

I was around ten or eleven years old, living in the projects in North Philadelphia on 2037 N. 11th Street, B floor, Apartment 12 a few days after Christmas when my mom told my siblings and me that our father was coming to visit. What was so ironic then was that I was so happy to know that this man, whom I had only heard about but had no memory of, was coming to visit us. What was even strange is that I felt an unshakable connection with this man right then and there and could not wait to see him.

As I prepared myself for his arrival, I thought about everything that he might say to us or do with us when he came over, or what I would say to him. Was he going to take us out? Or maybe he would hang around and play games with us for a while. The most important questions that flooded my mind were; *Where were you? Why did you leave us? Are you coming home to stay? Do you still love us? Do you still love Mommy?* So many questions I had as I, my sister, and brother anxiously awaited his coming. Then there was a knock on the door; it was as though he was knocking on my heart. My mom said, "It's your father." As we ran down the stairs, Mom gathered her keys to let my father in.

As the door opened wide, my heart swung open much wider, as it was filled with unrestrained excitement. Through the door walked in a tall, dark, lean and handsome man who greeted my siblings and me by name. It made me so happy just to hear my father greet us by our names.

In my excitement, I began to show him the drum set I'd gotten for Christmas. But I did not receive the type of response that I thought I should have received from him. Instead, he said to me in the most uncaring and nonchalant voice, "That's nice... Put it away. I'm talking to your mom right now." His response hurt me, so I replied in the most defiant way I could by saying, "NO!" He repeated himself several times, and I responded each time with the same answer.

I was hurt because I took his response as though he wasn't interested in me; forget what I was showing him. This man had abandoned me for years, and the only thing he could say was, "That's nice... Put it away. I'm talking to your mom right now..." I felt he could at least have shown a little more interest in what I was showing him, with a little more attention to me. But he didn't; instead, he hurt me to my core.

He became tired of repeating himself and said to my mom, "Rose, tell him something before I whoop his ass."

Concerned for my safety, my mom politely asked me to go upstairs. I complied, my eyes swelling with tears. I remember looking at him with much disdain and hurt in my heart. Nevertheless, I heeded my mother's warning and started my ascension upstairs. I was destroyed emotionally by a man that I barely knew, yet I longed for this man's attention and was traumatized when I didn't get it.

I felt rejected; I ran upstairs before my father had a chance to whoop me, but I could not move fast enough to escape the lashing that rejection left on my heart. The feeling of rejection so engulfed me; it seemed as though it was just him and me in that room, even though my brother and sister were there too.

As fathers, we must safeguard our children from the crippling effects of rejection by being careful with our words. Some children are dealing with the impact of rejection long after their father and mother have separated. Children are often so emotionally sensitive when parents break up that anything a parent does or say may be construed as rejection, even if that was not the intent. We must make sure that our being non-residential doesn't translate to non-involvement, but to empathetic involvement.

The second time I remember seeing my father took place not long after the first. This time it was impossible for him to give me the attention I desired from him. This time, I came to see him because he could not come to see me. This

24

time would be the last time that I would lay eyes on him. This time, that tall, dark and handsome man that I saw walking through those doors not so long ago laid lifeless before the eyes that he once filled with tears. But this time, there were no tears. In his death, he had taken to his grave any chance that I had to get to know him and for him to get to know me, so I thought. Yet, at that time, no tears were shed because I felt no loss for this man; I felt no rejection from him either.

How could I lose something I never had? How could I feel rejected by someone who I felt had no affection for me? As I sat in that funeral home, I tried to fit in with other family members that were there, crying because of their loss; but no matter how hard I tried to cry, I could not.

It was as though they knew my father in a way that I never knew him, in a way that every child should know their dad, with fond and pleasant memories. It was as if they had the memories of him that were supposed to be *my* memories, memories that would somehow be my inheritance. But I was left with nothing, nothing to reminisce about, no good or bad times on which to reflect. They were not memories that were erased; they just never existed. Like memories of my dad going to a sports event with me. Memories of him teaching me how to ride a bike. Memories of him holding my hands. Memories of him helping me with my homework. Memories of him holding me or caressing my cheeks when I was sad. No memories that warranted my tears, not that time. The father that I longed for had died.

As I sat in front of his coffin, I had only a yearning to have known him better, so that I could cry like everyone else was crying. Now, here he lay, lifeless in front of me in a coffin, without the ability to redeem himself from the blunder of abandonment, from not becoming the father he could have been; without the chance to explain why he wasn't. Death had robbed him of the opportunity to make right the wrong that he had done to my siblings and me. As a father, I know now that I can hurt my children more in life than I can by my death because they will remember the quality of our interactions together. But I also know that if the death of a child's father does not hurt that child, that father may have hurt them when he was alive.

Again, will your children be able to reminisce about you after you're gone? Will they be able to remember the times you spent playing with them? Will they have memories of times that made them laugh, as well as times that made them sad? Will they cherish the memories of the things you've said to them that brought them through situations? Will the life you lived evoke memories that will usher them through life's corridor, coming back to them like re-runs of their favorite TV show?

Will your words of wisdom guide them to a destination of success? Will they have unwanted memories of you or no memories at all? What good is there about you that they would want to emulate? Or will they remember and emulate the fears, poor self-esteem, hate, bigotries and other destructive ways that could represent the worst of you? Those ways that we know are wrong, but that we hold onto because we feel they preserve our existence, only leaving the future bleak and unsettling. These questions are why I encourage every non-residential father to allow your children to see how you live.

Let them see how you succeed in life. Let them see your work ethic. Let them see how you handle disappointments and adversities. Let them see how you treat people with respect and goodness, how you interact with your community and the communities of others. Most importantly, let them see how you treat their mother with respect, goodness and kindness, even though you two are no longer together. When they are older and long after you have passed, their memories of you will have a positive effect on the way they live and on the choices they make. Watching your life will have a strong influence on how they relate to, interact with, and raise their children. For what they see you do will live in them way longer than the things you've said to them in life.

Non-residential fathers should be such an intricate part of their children's lives to the extent that their children will not have time to miss them. Fathers have been out of sight, out of mind and out of touch with their children and communities. Thus, they are leaving behind a legacy of children who are out of control and not in touch with themselves and those around them.

As fathers, free or bound, rich or poor, famous or unknown, handy at or handicapped, regardless of wherever you are in life and whatsoever circumstances have come your way, you are still a father. Nothing on earth but you can ever change that. What traces of fatherhood will you leave behind? What kind of evidence of your existence will there be? Will they miss you? Or will they say, "Oh well, he didn't mean anything to me anyway!" or "I barely knew him." When you die, what will you leave behind for your children to reminisce about you?

We must leave our children with tools that they can use, which will help them navigate through this life. We must fill them with faith, self-esteem, good judgment, generosity, love and respect for themselves and others. We must show them how to persevere through times of failure. If we leave our children with these qualities, we will leave behind those who will uplift fallen communities from the plummeting of humanity. We will leave this world with those who will dream new dreams for the future. They will be good mothers and fathers of their time and will give birth to good mothers and fathers of future generations— all because we answered the call to fatherhood.

There is a great cause in which all of us—women and men, young and old—need to be engaged in; encouraging men to be involved fathers, and connecting all fathers with their children.

This is a struggle against an invisible foe—fathering deprivation. It's no exaggeration to say that every future generation depends on how we respond to this opportunity. ~ Dr. Ken R. Canfield, President of the National Center for Fathering, Speaker and Author of "The Heart of a Father," "The 7 Secrets of Effective Fathers," and "They Call Me Dad."

Chapter 6:

THE REASON

One day, I received a letter in the mail from Jackie, my father's sister's daughter. The letter said that she searched me out via the internet and that she and her mother, Rosita, (my father's only sibling) would like to meet me, my sister and brother. At the end of the letter were their address and contact information. After talking it over with my brother, we thought it would be a good idea to meet them. So, we called them and scheduled a day and time to get together; unfortunately, my sister couldn't be there because she lived in Washington DC at the time.

I'll never forget the day we met and the looks on their faces. There she was a small-framed elderly lady standing on the sidewalk, accompanied by an elderly gentleman. Both of them looked like two kids watching the ice cream truck coming down the street. As I drove by, and our eyes met. She then pointed at me and said, "That's him. I know it. He looks just like him."

The look on their faces became more indescribable as my brother and I stepped out of the truck and started walking towards them. Tears filled her eyes, with a look that said this was the only thing she had ever wanted in her life. We greeted them with hugs and kisses. The elderly gentleman was her husband; he also was my father's best friend. They welcomed us into their home, and as we sat inside and got acquainted with each other, they began telling us many stories about our father, some of which made me laugh, others that made me sad. I assumed these stories had the same effect on my brother as well. Out of all the stories they told us about our father, there were two that stuck out the most and forever changed the way I felt and thought about the father I barely knew.

One of those stories was about some family quarrel that took place between my mother and my father's side of the family. Because of what took place, my mother and my father's sister's relationship was severed entirely, and we were kept away from my dad's side of the family.   But the most compelling story was about my father being an alcoholic; it was his excessive out of control drinking that contributed to his improprieties, womanizing and the physical abuse to which he had subjected my mom. But as we all know, there are always factors even deeper than alcohol that are contributors to such behavior. Then, my aunt Rosita shared something that I never knew, something left out of all the things that I had ever heard about my father. When I heard it, it filled me with much sorrow, hope, and closure, all at the same time.

Aunt Rosita revealed to us how and why my father died. She let us know that it was his addiction to alcohol that played a major part in his abusive behavior toward my mother, his abandoning of his children, his promiscuity and many other bad choices. Aunt Rosita told us that our dad wanted so bad to come back to his family. However, he was an alcoholic and knew his return would be unsuccessful if he'd only repeated the same mistakes, and worse if he was still addicted to the same habits that played a role in ruining his marriage and his relationship with his children. That led him to do something drastic to speed up his hopeful return; my dad decided to go cold turkey. That decision cost him his life. The doctor told my aunt that because he was such a heavy drinker and was that for many years, going cold turkey shocked his systems, in particularly his immune system. The doctor told her that he would not have died if he had placed himself in a program and slowly weaned himself off the drinking.

My eyes filled with tears, and I realized at that very moment that regardless of what my father's demons were, whatever his weaknesses were, whatever his imperfections were, I sat on that sofa, realizing that his love for use was greater than those things. I realized just how much my dad loved us. At that moment, I finally understood that sometimes the wrong a person has done to you in one way or another, might have nothing to do with their love for you. Sometimes people are caught in the grips of their demons which make them unable to show love; the grips are so strong that they can't break loose.

Hearing that story made up for all the years I didn't see him; it made up for that one day he visited years ago after Christmas. The tears I didn't shed at his funeral finally came forth from my heart right then. I saw my dad from a different perspective, one that at that moment gave me a reason to feel for this man. I began to think about what our lives with him could have been. Hearing this story confirmed just how much he loved us.

Good or bad, do you remember who your father was? Understand that there is bad in the best of us and good in the worst of us. Take the good and bad things that you've seen in your father and use them both as lessons to help develop your relationship with your children. The question then becomes: what part of these experiences do we allow to affect our lives and our children's lives? Will they play a dominant role in the formation of our children's spiritual, emotional and mental stability? In what way? Will our choices fill them with quality teaching moments? When you encounter bad times, what will they remember about how you handled them? What reason would your children have to remember you? Or would you have given them no reason at all to want to remember you?

Don't leave your children with the only two memories that I had as a child of my dad before I met his sister; the day he hurt me and the day he died. Leave them with the knowledge that I had after talking with my aunt: that he loved me. This is the reason why we live: to leave our children with

33

hope in love and positive memories that will impact their lives for a lifetime. In the long run, they are the reasons why we do what we do... because it's all about them.

Chapter 7:

OBSTACLES BRING MIRACLES

Sam, who is a good friend of mine, would always say to me with a confident smile on his face, "Mingo, obstacles bring miracles." Powerful words that came back to me during the most trying times of my life as a man and father. I thank Sam for drilling those words into my subconscious, which always manifested themselves in my time of need. As this mantra was given to me, I feel it is my obligation to pass those powerful words of wisdom to every non-residential father, for indeed, obstacles bring miracles. I do not judge who or where you are in life. Regardless of life circumstances and obstacles, they should not keep you from the rewarding pursuit of fatherhood.

There will be a significant number of obstacles, and you may question if being an involved father in your children's life is all worth it. It is when those thoughts arise that I encourage you to look at any photos you may have of your children, see the smiles on their faces, see the innocence in their eyes, and therein lies your answer. Pictures of your children are excellent motivators to inspire you to press on with fatherhood. Sometimes we have to focus on reasons that are greater than ourselves to inspire us to go on; there is no reason more significant than our children. Being committed to the pursuit of fatherhood is worth it, even when confronted with obstacles.

A father's greatest success is only measured by the kind of father he was successful at being, not just by having the title of father. Though you may not live physically with your children, you are as much a part of their lives as the mother living with them. It is also a fallacy to think that just because a father doesn't live with his children, it makes him less important or less successful at fatherhood than fathers who live with their children.

No stepfather can take your place. There is no "stepfather" if you have never stepped out of your children's lives. That person may be the new husband of your child's mother (your ex) and someone with whom your child can hopefully develop a good relationship with. Ice cream isn't the only good thing that comes in double scoops. However, that person has not stepped into your place as a father because you have not stepped out of your parental role, and hopefully, you never will.

It is a difficult task being a non-residential father because it comes with many kinds of added pressures and often comes accompanied by feelings of guilt and inadequacy, mostly because you're not physically there with your children. One major obstacle is when fathers always argue with their exes, especially when they do this around the children. Fathers and mothers must learn to overcome these obstacles by not arguing and being vindictive in the presence of their children. No amount of money can give the emotional, mental and spiritual stability needed for a child when they have vindictive parents and are subject to seeing such vindictiveness. Children must see unity between parents, even when there is no more unity; children with parents who live together must see the same thing. They need to see collaboration between both parents, even if they are no longer together. As a non-residential father, you must be vigilant, relentless, persistent and creative in the way you pursue fatherhood when dealing with obstacles and circumstances. The task will not always be easy, but it is a possible task, and the reward will far outweigh the uneasiness of the task.

You're going to face some difficult times, frustrations and seemingly insurmountable obstacles. But obstacles bring miracles. Obstacles bring opportunities that teach us and make us mature. They give birth to wisdom and judgment and carry with them the opportunities to be overcomers; we only have to open our intuitive eyes to see those opportunities. As a father, you must choose proper actions when dealing with the obstacles of life; avoiding them is not an option, always keeping your goal in front of you: to be the best father you can for your children.

Chapter 8:

FINANCE VS. FATHERHOOD

Finances and/or the lack thereof is one of those obstacles you're going to face; probably the biggest situation non-residential fathers or any father will have to face. The society we live in has placed all too much emphasis on child support as the greatest solution for a failed marriage or relationship. Don't get me wrong, child support is necessary (and we will explore that topic in detail later), but it is not the essential thing a non-residential father should or can do. You may have sufficient funds, a low paying job or no job at all. Neither situation nullifies or voids your role as a father. Nor should anyone deny you of your involvement in your child's life because those things, for one has nothing to do with the other.

As I said, a man's financial stability or instability does not qualify nor disqualify him from being a good father. However, access to his financial stability makes life easier for the child and custodial parent. For instance, you may pay child support and never miss a payment, but not pay attention to spending quality time with or failing to invest in your children's emotional, mental, and spiritual well-being, ultimately leaving them in an emotional, mental and spiritual deficit. Often children will not even know they're in this emotional, mental or spiritual deficit until they've reached adulthood and have children of their own. But by then, they will be well-overdrawn in their attempts to make things work, wondering why their relationships are in the red emotionally, mentally and spiritually, even though they are financially in the black.

Faithful commitment to this financial obligation (child support) does not ensure emotional, mental or spiritual stability, nor does it make you or me good fathers. It is when we are fully invested in the lives of our children that we will enrich their lives and see positive returns.

In this western society, we find it so hard to conceive that money does not make a man successful at fatherhood, nor does it make a woman successful at motherhood. What this society has successfully done is put parenthood in the strangling grips of capitalism, where money controls the narrative of everything, even parenting. Capitalism, or what I call overtly extreme capitalism, has controlled the philosophy and changed the basic definitions, principles and concepts of how we parent and what it means to be a parent. Money has never replaced the benefits of an involved father and his influence on his children.

The adverse effects of fatherlessness are the same for every economic level. It does not discriminate whether or not a father is rich or poor. Money cannot replace the valuable influence of a hands-on father. And it never will. We must show our children that they are worth more than our money. What we do and the benefits they receive from us, and we from them, are worth so much more than dollars and cents.

There were times when my daughters would call me to ask if I could take them out. Often those times came when I had very little money, but I would go to my change jar (we all have a change jar) and gather just enough money so they could, at least, order from the dollar menu at McDonald's, or buy a water ice. There were times I've even borrowed money so that I could take my daughters out. I could have easily succumbed to feelings of shame and said that I couldn't do it that day, but I realized it wasn't about spending my money on them; they just wanted to spend time with me. My broke times (which were times when I had very little to no money) were some of the most rewarding and beautiful times that I spent with my girls.

Sometimes we're so depressed about having just a few dollars in our pockets that we choose to do nothing, when in reality, there is plenty we can do. You'll be surprised at what a few dollars and quality time will bring to your relationship with your children. Life with your children doesn't have to be empty just because your pockets are empty. The fullness of your relationship with your children can be enjoyed, even though your pockets aren't full.

Don't allow money or the lack of it to cloud your judgment. You can always get money back, but missed time and opportunity with your children, you can never get back. Missed time and opportunities with your children once squandered, are lost forever. It's not a sin to be a father with lots of money and to share it with your kids. It's a good thing. The sin comes in when you spend money as a substitute for *spending quality time* with your children. The best thing is to have lots of memories that you've shared together. Likewise, it's no sin to have only a few bucks in your pocket. The sin comes in when you use the lack of money as an excuse for not being involved with your children.

Time costs nothing, but it's the most precious and valuable thing we have in life. Fathers, rich or poor, are equally rich in the time they have to spend with their children. The real measure of a father's wealth is how much he'd be worth to his children if he would lose all his money.

Here are a few creative ideas that I've had with my girls that cost me little to nothing to do. Feel free to try them out with your children. I purposely left out the expensive things so that every non-residential father, no matter if they're rich or poor, can spend valuable time with their children. It is my purpose to take money out of the equation of the time we spend with our children. Money has blinded us to what is truly important in life. We often view and associate money with being successful or being the best at something. I cannot emphasize enough that you can spend quality time with your children with little to no money. The worth of a loving, involved relationship with your children is priceless!

CREATIVE IDEAS:

• **Shop in thrift stores:** When my girls were young, they loved shopping at thrift shops. I've even taken my girls to dollar stores and boy did they enjoy it! I made sure that I had at least $30-$50 to spend there. Each received $10 from me: I told them to buy whatever they wanted and something they needed.

• **McDonald's Dollar Menu:** Ten or twenty dollars can feed a few mouths with this option.

• **Walk and talk, communication is free:** Sometimes, I would ask my ex if it was ok for me to stop by and spend 30 minutes to 1 hour just talking to them and them talking to me. It's an excellent opportunity to go for a walk and to talk about things like school, personal problems and other things that may be on their minds. For this situation, you have to forge a good working relationship with your ex. Remember, it costs nothing to talk: communication is free.

• **Make family projects fun:** You can spend time washing your car with them. Even older kids enjoy doing this. Or help putting together a piece of equipment. Or mow the lawn, etc.

• **The Free Library:** Where the world is at your fingertips.

You may have a few ideas of your own, so write three ideas that you can do with your children that require little to no money. Write them below and use them the next time you're with your children.

1._____

_____

_____

_____

_____

_____

2._____

_____

_____

_____

_____

_____

_____

3._____

_____

_____

_____

_____

_____

_____

A truly rich man is one whose children run into his arms when his hands are empty.

- Author Unknown

Chapter 9:

THE STORY OF THE PRODIGAL RELATIONSHIP

Spending quality time with your children is better than spending quantities of money on them. The following epic biblical story illustrates the conflict between finance and fatherhood, between privilege and parenting. It's a compelling story of what can happen when a parent (a father in this case) cherishes and is more attentive to things than his children.

Jesus continued: 'There was a man who had two sons. The younger one said to his father, 'Father, give me my share of the estate.' So, he divided his property between them. Not long after that, the younger son got together all he had, set off for a distant country and there squandered his wealth in wild living. After he had spent everything, there was a severe famine in that whole country, and he began to be in need. So, he went and hired himself out to a citizen of that country, who sent him to his fields to feed pigs. He longed to fill his stomach with the pods that the pigs were eating, but no one gave him anything. When he came to his senses, he said, 'How many of my father's hired servants have food to spare, and here I am starving to death! I will set out and go back to my father and say to him: Father, I have sinned against heaven and against you. I am no longer worthy to be called your son; make me like one of your hired servants.' So, he got up and went to his father. But while he was still a long way off, his father saw him and was filled with compassion for him; he ran to his son, threw his arms around him and kissed him. The son said to him, 'Father, I have sinned against heaven and against you. I am no longer worthy to be called your son.' But the father said to his servants, 'Quick! Bring the best robe and put it on him. Put a ring on his finger and sandals on his feet. Bring the fattened calf and kill it. Let's have a feast and celebrate. For this son of mine was dead and is alive again; he was lost and is found.' So, they began to celebrate. Meanwhile, the older son was in the field. When he came near the house, he heard music and dancing. So, he called one of the servants and asked him what was going on. 'Your brother has come,' he replied, 'and your father has killed the fattened calf because he has him back safe and sound.' The older brother became angry and refused to go in. So, his father went out and pleaded with him. But he answered his father, 'Look! All these years I've been slaving for you and never disobeyed your orders. Yet you never gave me even a young goat so I could celebrate with my friends. But when this son of yours who has squandered your property with prostitutes comes home, you kill the fattened calf for him!' 'My son,' the father said, 'you are always with me, and everything I have is yours. But we had to celebrate and be glad, because this brother of yours was dead and is alive again; he was lost and is found.'-Luke 15:11-32

Allow me to take this well-known biblical story and attempt to tell it in a way that it has never been told before. It is a compelling story about a very wealthy father and his two sons, a younger son and an older son. What's even more compelling was the difference in the kind of relationship he had with each of them. This father's relationship with his sons said more about the father than it did his sons. If you read very carefully, you will see that this story is not just about a wayward son who wasted his inheritance, money and resources on extravagant reckless living. But it is a story about a father who paid more attention to and who allowed his money, resources and lavish lifestyle to distract him from his son.

We can surmise by the subtle and not so subtle actions and reactions of the characters in this story the type of relationship they had with one another. As I read and carefully studied the actions and reactions, the responses and non-responses of all the parties involved in this story, this father gave both sons whatever they wanted, whenever they wanted it. He thought his riches and things could replace his time and attention. But the father's attention was the one thing that the older son got a lot of, but the younger son did not. Money and wealth were all this father had to offer the younger son, at least for a time.

As you see, this father was a very successful entrepreneur, businessman, go-getter, a leader in the community and innovator of new ideas who possessed leadership skills, management ability and team-building capabilities. Though he possessed all these qualities that made for a great businessman, it hindered him from being the attentive father that he should have been. He was unable to transition these qualities to become a good attentive father. As mentioned earlier, his relationship with each son was entirely different, in that he had a much more attentive relationship with the older son than he did with the younger son. This father's actions were not meant to be purposely dismissive of the younger son, but partly was more based on genetics in that traditionally in those days, fathers would prep the older son for the future takeover of the family business and estate. This required that a father spent a considerable amount of time with the oldest son when he reached a certain age, showing the son the ends and outs of the business, introducing the son to and getting him acquainted with the business partners, cronies and other vital connections through attending business conventions, social events or playing board games. So naturally, because of this, most of the father's time, interaction, attention and involvement were given to the older son.

Most likely, this made the younger son feel like a fatherless child and he longed for the same attention that he saw his brother receive from their father. This son was suffering from the effects of what I call Attention Deprivation. Attention Deprivation is when a child is deprived of the necessary attention needed from a parent that's required for that child to thrive and grow emotionally, mentally and spiritually. The damaging effects and misleading symptoms of

Attention Deprivation can make the victim (the child) seem as though they are the problem and that something is wrong with them. When, in fact, it is the parent that is the problem.

When parents do not give their children the necessary attention that's needed for them to thrive, a child may display negative behaviors to get the attention they've been craving. Society will misdiagnose the child as being a bad kid and prescribe the wrong prescription for that child (like prison) when the only antidote is the attention of a loving father. But we must not be misled to think the older son was in a better position than the younger son, for though he got all the fathers' attention, it was given for self-serving reasons. This attention was given so that the legacy of the father might continue. This only further showed how this father's blinding ambition and lofty goals had prevented him from seeing the damage that he was causing, and from seeing what was truly important in life.

This father failed to give the younger son anything that resembled the loving attention of a father, with each passing day being a day lost to spent with his younger son. The son became famished for his father's attention, and became willing to do whatever it took to satisfy the hunger. So, the son cooked up an outrageous scheme that he thought would surely get his father's attention and get him to notice him, just as much as he did the older son.

He went on to make an unusual request of his father. The son insisted that the father give him his share of the estate. This share of the estate was probably part of his father's will, only given to his children upon his death. This younger son figured such a request would spark his father to pay a little more attention to him.

Jesus continued: 'There was a man who had two sons. The younger one said to his father, 'Father, give me my share of the estate.' So, he divided his property between them." - - Luke 15:11-12

Without his father's attention, this son had no father with whom to talk, and no father that could help him through tough times or even know that he was going through tough times. He had no father who could give him answers to life's many questions. He had no father with whom to engage in any social activities or just "shoot the breeze".

With all his father's attention given to the older brother, the younger son felt rejected and dejected. So, he thought this outlandish premature request would surely get his apathetic father to notice him, but it didn't. The father was so out of touch that he didn't even pay attention to the unusualness of the son's request. He was so out of touch with his younger son's need for his attention that he gave him the things that he thought would make him happy. He gave him possessions. He couldn't see that the only thing his son wanted was his father's attention.

The request should have been a red light for this father to stop and pay attention. And to put a halt to anything and everything with which he was preoccupied at that time. This request should've worried this father to the extent that he would have asked some pertinent questions like: "Why?" or "Son, is there something wrong? Are you in any trouble, son?" or "What's going on in your life that you need this inheritance now?" He didn't even take the time to ask his son anything or to sit and talk to him. No, that would require too much of this father's precious time.

The process of giving the younger son his inheritance probably took some considerable time. Giving him his portion of the inheritance, most likely consisted of giving him a substantial amount of money, dividing what part of the livestock and real estate property that he owned — and handing over deeds of ownership of these things, etc. In the time it took to do all that, it gave the father even more time to think about this unusual request of the son and make the appropriate response to it. But scripture never indicates any such things happening; instead, it merely suggested that the father just simply handed over to his son his inheritance, no question asked, without any hesitation whatsoever.

...So, he divided his property between them. - Luke 15:12b

Because the father's response was not the response the son had hoped for, the son took his scheme to phase two in the attempt to get his father's attention. Phase two was to become a runaway, to elope from the secured, yet inattentive environment of his father's house. The son probably thought to himself, *Since asking for all my inheritance didn't work, I'll run away from home; this will certainly get my father's attention. He will notice that I've packed all my belongings and that my room is empty; he'll drop everything he's doing and come looking for me.* Unfortunately, this runaway son and his empty room went unnoticed by this busy father. The son was gone for years, so long that he spent all his inheritance and even moved to another country. He probably thought that the longer he was away at some point, his father would send a search party out to look for him. No such luck. This confirmed, even more, the son's belief that his father didn't care about him the same way he cared about the older son.

Allow me to interject something before I continue with this story; that is this: this father's lack of attention towards his son was not an indication that he didn't love his younger son. He loved both his sons a lot. But it is an indication that his priorities were not in order. Priorities should be put in order according to the worth and importance of a thing.

For where your treasure is, there your heart will be also. -Matthew 6:21

When a man and woman have children, the importance and worth of every other thing takes a backseat to their child's growth and wellbeing. The importance of everything a parent does should be based around their children. We should see and treat them as God sees and treats them.

Behold, children are a heritage from the Lord, the fruit of the womb a reward. - Psalm 127:3

This scripture lets us know that our children are our prized possessions, our winnings, trophies, honor, decorations, legacy and inheritance from God. They are those who makes our lives more cheerful, lively and interesting if we treat and cherish them as such.

Let us continue with the story. So, the son began living a wild, wasted, and out of control life because of his need for and lack of his father's attention. So much so that at this point, anyone's attention would do. To make things worse, the country that he lived in was in a great depression.

This was a son who never had a need for anything except for his father's attention. Now he found himself in trouble, in need of the basic necessities of life, so much so that he took a job that was way below his standard of life: a job feeding pigs. This was the most condescending job there was, a job that didn't even pay him enough for him to make a decent living. He was so hungry that he contemplated eating the very same slop that he fed to the pigs. Because of his failed scheme, he found himself homeless and starving, a plan that was swirling out of control with outcomes that were never intended by this young man. Yet there was no one to help him, no one that cared and no one that would pay attention to his plight.

His scheme to get his father's attention had backfired and left him wanting and depraved. This son left a father who genuinely loved him, but who had his priorities in the wrong place. Instead his father prioritized people who had no love for him and who could care less about him. He knew his father was so well known; he just knew someone would recognize him and see how he was living and report back to his father when they saw his condition.

(vs13-16) *Not long after that, the younger son got together all he had, set off for a distant country and there squandered his wealth in wild living. After he had spent everything, there was a severe famine in that whole country, and he began to be in need. So, he went and hired himself out to a citizen of that country, who sent him to his fields to feed pigs. He longed to fill his stomach with the pods that the pigs were eating, but no one gave him anything.*

Not only did the unloving, cruel environment of the world bring this young man to his knees, but it brought him to his senses as well. He realized that he did not have to live like this; he did not have to be deprived of the necessities of life. He realized that his father was wealthy. But he knew that he had to ask for his father's forgiveness for wasting and exploiting the inheritance the father had given and for living a lifestyle that disgraced his father's name. His need for survival overrode his need for attention. This young man settled for living void of his fathers' attention over living a life deprivation. Ironically, sometimes a parent's neglect can force a child to have to choose from the lesser of two evils. Even though all his misdoings were an attempt to get his father's attention, he was still willing to ask for forgiveness and to become like one of his father's servants if need be. Besides, if no one cared that he was missing, they probably wouldn't notice when he returned.

(vs 17-20) *When he came to his senses, he said, 'How many of my father's hired men have food to spare, and here I am starving to death. I will set out and go back to my father and say to him: 'Father, I have sinned against heaven and against you. I am no longer worthy to be called your son; make me like one of your hired men.' So, he got up and went to his father...*

But boy, was this son surprisingly mistaken; as he made his way home, the father recognized him from a distance despite his thin famished frame.

(vs 21-24) But while he was still a long way off, his father saw him and was filled with compassion for him; he ran to his son, threw his arms around him and kissed him. The son said to him, 'Father, I have sinned against heaven and against you. I am no longer worthy to be called your son.' But the father said to his servants, 'Quick! Bring the best robe and put it on him. Put a ring on his finger and sandals on his feet. Bring the fattened calf and kill it. Let's have a feast and celebrate. For this son of mine was dead and is alive again; he was lost and is found.' So, they began to celebrate.

This father was so excited to see his son returning home that he ran to him, put his arms around him and kissed him despite the pungent stench of deprivation and ragged attire of a peasant. The fact that the father ran to his son, hugged him and kissed him, not even allowing the son time to ask for forgiveness, speaks volumes to this father's actions. He was not seeking a confession from his son; he was seeking his son's forgiveness. This father's actions were very similar to the actions of the woman who came to Jesus, wetting his feet with her tears and wiping them with the hair of her head, kissing his feet as she anointed them with expensive oil from an alabaster box, seeking forgiveness.

The father knew that this was not a time for reprimanding or judging his son for what he did and for the condition he was in. But instead, the father saw this as a second chance to make right his wrong, a second chance for him to be the father he should have been and an opportunity to give the son the attention he so longed and deserved. It was the father that he failed to be which ultimately played a major part in his son's condition. The father saw this as his second chance for reconciliation and rebuilding a longed lost relationship. Yes, those many years of his son's absence also gave this father time for retrospection and introspection. He saw the error of his ways, regretting not giving his son the attention due to him when he had a chance. The father that he should have been, he was now ready to be, and this was evident in the attention he gave the son.

Even though the son looked quite different from the way he left, having suffered from the effects of a cruel world and the consequences of poor choices, the son made his way to his father. But the father didn't see those things; he did not see a wretched child. He didn't see the ugliness of what life had made him. He saw his son that needed his attention. And he knew that if he gave his son the attention that was denied him, it would be the one thing that would repair him. This father saw a second chance at fatherhood and was willing to pull out all the stops to pursue it, and he was determined not to mess up this chance again. You see, during the years of his son's absence, the father realized where he went wrong and would have given anything for a second chance to make right the wrong that he caused.

Not only was this a second chance for the father to give his son the attention he deserved, but it was a chance for everyone else to notice and pay attention to the son, acknowledging that this was indeed his son. So, he gave him a robe signifying his prestigious position in society. Though he did not look like the child he was before he left, this robe signified the father's desire to cover up the indiscretion with his prominent status and good standing in society. It was a statement to the community that despite what his son did, he was still *his* son. He was letting all the onlookers know, *What I am, he is. What I have, he has. When you respect me, he's worthy of that same respect.* Fathers are no greater than the status that they have with their children. Then the father put a ring on the son's finger, representing the father's new and undying devotion, faithfulness, and attentiveness to his son.

The father also gave the son sandals signifying that even though the son lived an unacceptable lifestyle, he was still worthy to walk in his father's shoes, shoes that would protect his feet as he walked through life's rough terrain and charted his own course in life. He also wanted the younger son to know that he doesn't have to be like the older son to receive his attention; the son could simply be himself and receive the same fatherly attention and care. This second chance for this father to build a loving relationship with his son was a reason for celebration. Likewise, any time we see God repairing the damaged relationship between a father and a child, any time we see that relationship start to come together just a little bit, it is a big reason to celebrate.

As you can see, this story was not just about a son who left home and behaved recklessly, but more about a father who was reckless with his priorities, which eventually drove his son away into a reckless lifestyle. We've read statistics of the negative impact it has on children when a father is not attentively involved in the lives of his children. And again, I must reiterate, just because a father lives with his children doesn't mean that he is involved with them, or that he's giving his children the attention that they need. This story is a prime example of that.

This story was not about a prodigal son; it was about a prodigal relationship. It wasn't about a lost son; it was about a lost relationship and the restoration of that relationship. It was more about how the drama in a son's life changed a father's mindset. It was about the change that took place in the lives of a son and his father. It was about a son going his own way and doing what he thought was necessary to get his father to pay attention to him. And about a father who almost lost a son because he did not see the necessity in giving his son the attention he needed, the right kind of attention. When our children act out, we as fathers need to make sure that we are not the cause of our children acting unseemingly.

If you read carefully, you can see the contrast in the attention given to the son before he left compared to when he returned. In reading this story, we know why this father gave his son so much attention after the son returned home in this depraved condition. We now know why the father didn't give the son that same kind of attention when he lived with him. It was like we were looking at a before and after photo of these two characters in this story. Why this drastic change? The simple answer to this question is that conditions and circumstances sometimes make us do things that we shouldn't do. Yet, somehow the consequences of what we do have a way of changing us for the better.

Chapter 10:

FORGIVENESS

When our children genuinely come to their senses, fathers should be there with loving arms to welcome them back and forgive them. Forgiveness is not only about forgiving a person for what they've done, but it is about showing compassion and kindness to a person despite what they've become. When a person forgives, it says more about the person giving forgiveness than it does about the person receiving forgiveness. Forgiveness is not compromising right for wrong, but the absence of forgiveness will compromise one's ability to fix the wrong and to respond appropriately to it.

Some people need one chance; some two or three; some need four and others even more. How many chances should we give our children? I can only say this, that any chance after the last chance may be the very one chance they needed.

Forgiveness must take place between both parents responsible for bringing a child into the world. Mothers are quicker to forgive the deeds of a wayward child than fathers are. Women are usually even more forgiving of wayward husbands. But men, generally find it harder to forgive. In some cases, we might forgive, but *we ain't never gonna forget*. We might say we forgive, but there won't be no coming back from the wrong committed. We'll forgive, but that forgiveness will come with some conditions. Conditions like, if they don't find a job in a week, they're out. Or making sure the bathroom and living room are clean every day, mowing the lawn, shovelling snow, washing the car, babysitting your siblings for free, coming in with an early curfew, and no visitation from friends for a long while. And, if the child disagreed or failed to meet these conditions, a father may not let his child return. Yes, it is a little exaggerated, but you get the picture. Some of these are not unreasonable conditions and are sometimes necessary to teach responsibility. But if left by themselves and not coupled with the loving attention of a father, these only become vindictive, spiteful measures. Most times, we as men feel that we use logic more than emotions. But in some situations, being logical isn't the best thing to be.

As fathers, we must learn to forgive. We must become a student of forgiveness, along with our exes, in-laws and grandparents. Even our children must become students of forgiveness. However, forgiveness starts with you, the father; and you must practice forgiveness even if the other parties involved don't. Forgiveness opens the doors to solutions and bonding, and puts all parties involved on the path of a common purpose. That common purpose can result in a vibrant and renewed relationship, as well as the healthy well-being of our children.

Children need to forgive their fathers and not hold animosity in their hearts. Hatred and unforgiveness are cancerous, and like cancer, they will ultimately eat away at everything to which it attaches itself. Fathers must forgive the father that hurt them in order to break the cycle of unforgiveness from spreading to their children. Forgiveness frees us from displaced anger that can hinder us from having a meaningful relationship with our children and with others. Forgiveness makes you a better person, even if that person whom you forgave is not a better person. It is not only the absence of a father that contributes to the statistics we talked about earlier, but the anger, hate and animosity children hold for that father that can send them into a destructive lifestyle.

When we forgive, it helps us to find a way out of our problems, and we begin to make declarations that organize our lives in a way that will bring about change. A change that will not only benefit us, but will cause a shift in our country, communities and children. A father, who has not been involved in his children's lives but wants to get involved, must be patient with a child who is slow to forgive. A father's absence and non-activity can cause a lot of pain and resentment in his children; they will need time to heal from the hurts. Give them that time, allow them the space that's required for them to pursue forgiveness.

Chapter 11:

TO BE OR NOT TO BE A FATHER?

To be a father or not to be a father? This shouldn't be a question or decision to make for any man who is partly responsible for bringing children into this world. We, as men, should not find it hard to perform the essential role as a father. We didn't find it hard doing what it took to make a child, did we? Not even animals find it difficult playing their natural roles as parents; it comes naturally, and they embrace it. Then why do humans have problems with performing their fundamental functions of parenting? Why do we have issues embracing this role?

Mothers should embrace their natural role as mothers and fathers should embrace their role as fathers. We even have problems embracing our natural role as husband and wife; this is because there are systems set in place in this society that make it unacceptable, difficult and belittling for a man and woman to embrace their natural roles. That's a topic for another book. Being a father is a great thing, a gift, a treasure of incalculable value, a high calling and our utmost responsibility, and so is being a mother. When fathers and mothers, men and women, don't embrace their natural roles in the script of life, the story never goes well, bad ratings ensured.

I give much respect to those fathers who still live with their children. But while this is the perfect scenario, it is not always reality. Just because a father lives under the same roof as his children doesn't mean that that father is actively involved with his children. Involvement is the responsibility of every father regardless of where they live or don't live.

It is ludicrous to think that the term "good father" is only reserved for those fathers who live with their children. There are approximately 24 million children who live in homes without their biological fathers. That means that one out of every three children do not live under the same roof with their father. What those statistics do not tell us is how many of those children who live under the same roof with their father enjoy the loving, active involvement of that father; this knowledge will skew those statistics dramatically — just something to think on.

Fathers are not without imperfections, but not even our flaws are excuses for us not being actively involved in our children's lives. Our imperfections should be the reason we pursue betterment in our lives. With that said, we must be careful of the shortcomings that we allow our children to see.

Some things we do as adults are not necessarily wrong or sinful, but are things that our children should not see, hear or taste. Some things should be reserved for adulthood. Even then, we must be prudent of what we allow them to see us do.

A father's relationship with his children is not, nor should it be the same type of relationship that the child has with their peers (associates of equal standing like classmates or friends). Being a father goes much deeper and should be more influential. Our actions must be exemplary in the call of fatherhood. The relationship between a father and his children may have friend-like qualities of a more profound sense. Being a father is much more than being a friend, crony or a homie; its difference is as different as being in the lobby of a five-star hotel compared to being in the penthouse.

If you do not have the relationship you want with your children, keep trying. If you're going to be a father, then be a father. If you want things to happen, then make them happen. Situations can change if you want them to change and are willing to put in the time and effort to bring about change. Never stop seeing the possibilities. Stop striving to recapture what could have been; instead, seize the time to capture the *now*. Put fatherhood before all other things. The pursuit of fatherhood will push you to pursue a better life for yourself.

Non-residential fathers, as well as at-home fathers who are seeking to be better fathers should pursue a better civil working relationship with the mother of their children. A good relationship between mother and father is just as essential for divorced parents as it is for parents who are together. Because that children's mother is the other half of the equation to being an effectively involved father, the way you treat her, even though you are no longer together, and how you treat her will have an impact on your children's well-being. And vice versa.

You may not be a perfect sower, but you can sow the right seed. What you plant in your children's lives today will determine what they will grow to be tomorrow. We must give our children the tools they need to stand on their own feet, become independent while helping them make the right decisions, set goals and be the best they can be. We must do this even when we are not at our best. Not being at our best doesn't mean that we can't give them what is best for them. The truth is that children don't care about your imperfections. They are not worried about your failures; they want your involvement. They want you to be a father to them.

The North Carolina Cooperative Extension Service says, "Fathers play a key role in the successful socialization of children. Regardless of the marital status of the parents, the father needs to be actively engaged in his child's life, especially during the child's early years. Physical presence is not enough; he must be emotionally involved. Often, men don't know how to involve themselves effectively in the lives of their children, but they can learn. Consistent, positive interaction between fathers and children lowers the risk of many of the negative social and emotional impacts previously mentioned. Numerous studies have shown that fathers' availability and involvement reduce aggressive behavior in boys and enhance academic performance in both sons and daughters. Lack of a father's expressiveness and intimacy with their children appear to have the greatest long-term implications for children's development. The active father encourages independence, standing up for oneself and acceptance of one's mind, body and personality. Fathers play a huge role in nurturing their children and can foster creativity, a positive body image, moral standards and social competence."[1]

As I said before, we must eliminate even those "legitimate" reasons that we say are hindering us from being a father. There is no valid reason for this act of omission. If you are a father who is struggling with addiction, like drugs or alcohol, of course, it's not a good situation for your children to be around. But if you're a father battling an addiction, your will to be a father must rise above that addiction by pursuing whatever help needed for you to overcome your addiction and to pursue fatherhood. It would be best if you did this so that your children won't make the same poor choices you've made, decisions that ultimately led to your addiction. When you become addicted to fatherhood, you won't want to be addicted to those addictions anymore. Your high will become your children; your motivation to overcome and your dependencies will be your children.

---

[1] "Fathers," www.ces.ncsu.edu/depts/fcs/pdfs/Fcs-509.pdf, The North Carolina Cooperative Extension Service, 2018

It is statistically evident that the answer to the problems of our youth is not more laws, jails or institutions, but for more fathers to become active in their children's lives. We have built more prisons, institutions and developed many programs, yet we have not put a significant dent in the problems that plague our youth. We need more fathers engaging in the mental, emotional, spiritual and social well-being of their children. While other factors are keys to successfully rearing a child, the impact of a father's parenting cannot be minimized nor overlooked.

When fathers become actively involved in the lived of their children (not just physically present), it can potentially lower the school dropout rate, teenage murder rate, teen pregnancy rate, suicide and behavioral health problems.

Instead of spending tons of financial resources on prisons, police, juvenile facilities and family court systems, we should invest that money in a Father Support Association. This association would assist both at-home fathers and non-residential fathers, adult fathers, as well as teen fathers in the fundamentals of fatherhood through online classes, literature, seminars, social gatherings and counseling. Even though it would be Christian-based, the association would not refuse fundamental counseling to those who are dealing with life threatening, emotionally and mentally stressful issues who are not of the same faith. This association believes that it can address common fundamental problems that affect all fathers without compromising the conviction of their faiths. Fathers will also be able to attend support group sessions with other fathers.

The association will also focus on education, jobs, housing and offer vocational courses that non-residential fathers can take for free. Fathers must commit to this program for one year. After that one year, a mentor will be assigned to that father who will fellowship with him once or twice a month for another year. He will also have access to the organization when personal problems related to fathering occurs. An Annual Father Family Reunion will also be held, where fathers can bring their children to enjoy a day of fun, bonding and networking. This program will spring forth benefits that will last a lifetime. The Father Support Association would not only be funded by taxpayers' money, but also through donations from corporate America. This would not be an added tax, just a redistribution of taxes. If we can bail out corporate America from their wasted and irresponsible use of billions of dollars, then indeed we can help responsible and irresponsible fathers by giving them a second chance and the tools needed to become successful fathers.

We must first believe that in this sea of irresponsible fathers, there are fathers who want to do better (and there are). In some situations, a father's lack of involvement is not the fault of that father. Some blame should be placed on our society because it puts more importance on other things over our children. We are a capitalistic country, and in most cases, capitalism overrides and takes priority over the future and well-being of our children. This is unacceptable and must cease. We must look to make societal changes in this country if we truly want to deal with these issues. This program is essential for not only positive change in fathers, but in our children and communities. It is why I say:

FATHERHOOD IS THE MISSING LINK AND IS VITAL IF WE'RE SERIOUS ABOUT SOLVING SOCIAL, COMMUNAL AND ECONOMIC DEPRIVATION.

Institutions like the Boys & Girls Clubs of America™ and recreation centers are great avenues for our children, but they do not and cannot replace a father's worth. I am in no way coming down on these institutions; they are doing great work and have produced great success stories. But the institution of fatherhood is the highest institution of all, bar none. The impact that fatherhood can have on our society is immeasurable; it will yield a much bigger return than these establishments. These institutions should be a place where fathers can take their sons or daughters to bond with them. They should be a source that aid in the building and success of the child-parent relationship, not to take the place of that relationship. They should be a place that helps men to be fathers and women to be mothers.

Chapter 12:

LOCKED UP, THEY WON'T LET ME OUT

Again, *To be or not to be a father?* should not be a question. Maybe the question should be *How to be?* especially when posed by fathers who are incarcerated. Then we have fathers who, because of their criminal lifestyle and behaviors, have abandoned their children by way of the penal system. They find themselves in and out of prison or are serving a life sentence, yet the questions we should be asking ourselves is: Can a father be a positive influence in the lives of his children while being behind prison walls? And if you are an incarcerated father, do you believe that you can you still pursue fatherhood while looking through the bars of a cell? Can you reach out and touch the hearts, minds and souls of your offspring while incarcerated? My answer is yes, you can! You can take away a father's physical freedom, but he can still be free to pursue fatherhood while incarcerated.

Being a father can never be taken away from you unless you give it away. How unfortunate that would be. The role of fatherhood is not out of reach for incarcerated fathers; it is just as attainable as it is for free fathers. You may have different obstacles, but being a parent is still an achievable goal.

You may be locked up, but your influence as a father can't be restricted by that which confines you physically; your influence is free to roam wherever your children are. You may be behind bars, in chains and surrounded by insurmountable walls; none of these things can imprison the power of your words. From inescapable bars, walls and chains of incarceration, the power of your words can penetrate and touch the hearts and souls of your children. As diligently as one seeks an appeal, incarcerated fathers must pursue fatherhood with that same diligence, as though his life depended on it – or as though his children's lives depended on it.

This chapter is not meant to judge incarcerated fathers; they've been judged already, nor is it to condemn them; their actions have already condemned them. But this is to encourage incarcerated fathers to be proactive, despite what may seem to be an unrealistic task for someone in their predicament. Fathers in these predicaments must put all their focus on the pursuit of fatherhood. They must be committed fully to pursuing parenthood, so that their children wouldn't find themselves in the same condition. When a father's focus is 100% on becoming a better father, it will make him a better person, a better man.

When incarcerated fathers began to engulf themselves in the things that will make them better fathers, they will find real rehabilitation. An incarcerated father focusing on the well-being of his children is the greatest form of rehabilitation.

Being an involved father will be more difficult from where you're standing. It will require some extraordinary creativity on your part, but it can be done. It will be worth every effort, especially when you consider what could become of your children if you don't pursue fatherhood compared to what can become of them if you do. If people can obtain degrees, high school diplomas, write books, make money and even win the Nobel Peace Prize while incarcerated, surely a man can become successful at fatherhood from those same walls of confinement.

First, the work must be put in the painstaking task yet rewarding effort of rekindling the relationship with his children. Physical barriers may restrict you, but your involvement with your children is not, nor should it be defined by your environment, circumstances or mistakes. The life of your children can never be limited by those things. Your display of love for them can never be confined. Your loving participation in their lives will prevent them from being imprisoned emotionally, mentally and spiritually, serving out their lives on the streets of death row. How can this be done? Here is my acronym for *H.O.W.:*

Hard- Choosing to take on the task to be involved in the life of your children while incarcerated is not going to be an easy one; it's going to be hard. Difficult times are going to come;

stored up and unresolved emotion will be unleashed. I say *unleashed* because your children will let loose emotions of anger, sadness and regret of why you choose the thing that imprisoned you over them. Your response may be, *It wasn't about you* or *I did it all because of you.* Neither response may be acceptable for a child who longs for the physical presence of his or her father. At the same time, you may unleash your emotions of regret and guilt, but all emotions should be understood and forgiven in order to move forward successfully. When this is done, you will find the rewards will be greater than that which was unleashed- for your children and yourself.

Ongoing- It will take some time, but you must stay the course. Your perseverance is necessary to achieve the lofty rewarding task of fatherhood. The role of a father never ends; it must be continuous, without interruption or gaps and consistent to achieve maximum success. The effects and efforts of good parenting will live long after your life has ended. As an involved incarcerated father, your parenting can break the negative cycle that may be afflicting your family or a cycle that started with you. Physical barriers cannot hinder the positive influence of fatherhood, nor can it be confined by social walls when you use the power of loving involvement to chisel away at those emotional walls of disdain, hate, hurt and regret.

Work- Being an incarcerated father and maintaining involvement in your child's life will take action; it will take lots of practice. Fatherhood is a lifestyle, a calling and an obligation to a life. It requires no diploma, certifications or degrees to do the work, only a loving commitment. That's *H.O.W.* you become a successfully incarcerated father. So, let's get to work!

Incarcerated fathers should be encouraged to know that even though they are not able to participate in activities with their children like non-incarcerated fathers are, their words can be the most potent form of involvement used with their children. This is true in any relationship. We should never underestimate the power of our words, the changes that they can create and the constructive power as well as destructive power they have. Our words can inspire people to action or discourage them from implementing any action. Even the Bible illustrates the importance of words where it makes statements like *God spoke* or *Thus sayeth the Lord*, letting us know and warning us of what would happen if we do or don't heed His words.

But he said, 'On the contrary, blessed are those who hear the word of God, and keep it.' -Luke 11:28

When we hear the word of God, and we store and cherish it in our hearts, our hearts become a treasure chest of inspiration, and so is the inspiring words of the incarcerated parent to their children.

Your word is a lamp for my feet, and a light for my path. -Psalm 119:105

I want to say this to incarcerated fathers who might be reading this book: your words alone can become the navigation system that will lead your children to a better destiny and path of enlightenment.

The Bible also talks about the Word as the force that created all things. Such as the iconic passage of scripture where Jesus is called the Word *(John 1)*, the Bible further illustrates the power, position and ability of the Word to create something out of nothing.

In the beginning was the Word, and the Word was with God, and the Word was God. The same was in the beginning with God. All things were made by him; and without him was not any thing made that was made. -John 1:1-3

In a like manner, your words can create a new relationship and new beginnings between you and your children, despite the walls and bars that separate you. Words inhaled through congestive nostrils of hopelessness, then passed down through the trachea of perseverance, purified of the toxicity of doubt and fear as it passes through the respiratory system of faith and prayer; then hopefulness is exhaled into the souls of our children, creating actions of faith that will allow them to create new landscapes for their lives, much different from the one you've created for yourself *(Mark 11:22-24)*.

In both at-home fathers or non-residential fathers, our words are important. What we speak to our children and our circumstances will determine their outcome. We can speak words of life, or we can speak words of death to them. We can choose to speak of and talk about things that result in life by using what I call the Ezekiel Effect. The Ezekiel Effect essentially is when the circumstances of life or the relationship with our children seem fatal, and we use words of affirmation, inspiration and rejuvenation to bring new life to them. Although there are those relationships and circumstances that are better off left dead, as in the relationship with an ex, the Bible gives an awe-inspiring illustration of the power of words and how they can be used as affirmation, inspiration and rejuvenation, applying them to seemingly hopeless situations, breathing life into them. The end results of our words are determined by the words we use. This illustrative example is found in Ezekiel 37:1-10, where God shows Ezekiel a vision of a valley full of dry bones.

In this passage of scripture, God gave Ezekiel a vision of a valley of dry decaying bones and used it as a metaphor for a hopeless condition. Five things took place in that vision:

1. God put Ezekiel smack dab in the middle of the current condition. God doesn't want us on the outskirts of our problems. God wants us to stop running away from seemingly hopeless situations and start running to them. Sometimes life seems hopeless, dead, and despondent, but it is what we speak to and where we are standing at in those times that will determine our outcome or how we come out.

...the Spirit of the Lord and set me in the middle of a valley...- Ezekiel 37:1

2. Not only did God put Ezekiel in the middle of the valley of dry bones, but he had Ezekiel to do a walkthrough. It's not enough to notice the devastation of our children, community, and society as we are settled idly while doing nothing. We must get involved. We must not only run to and stop running from our current situations, but we must work from the inside out, involving ourselves in the process of the solution. Many adults see what's wrong, but do

nothing to become the solution to what they see, not seeing that their acts of omission are as much of the causes of the things they see are wrong. You have to walk through the devastation, engage yourself in your current circumstance and get into the mix. As fathers, we can no longer stand on the outside and view the problems facing our children; we cannot just be observers from afar, or stand idly in the middle doing nothing. We must be present and engaging, we must walk through the carnage of the present, lifted by our past. We must put ourselves in the midst of and engage in our current situations to evaluate what we see and that which we seek to change.

He led me back and forth among them, and I saw a great many bones on the floor of the valley, bones that were very dry. - Ezekiel 37:2

3. Then God asked a question.

He asked me, 'Son of man, can these bones live?'- Ezekiel 37:3

This vision is also a testament of when things seem done, and it seems impossible to bring life to your situations and circumstances, when you think it's impossible for things to get any better because it's been that way for a long time, God asks and cares about how we feel. He cares about your opinions, your fears, doubts, and the uncertainty of the future of your current situations.

4. Then after hearing our fears, doubts and uncertainties, and opinions God tells us to do something, something contrary to what we see. God told Ezekiel to speak to the bones. How can you speak to something that's dead? but that's exactly what God told Ezekiel to do.

Then he said to me, 'Prophesy to these bones and say to them, 'Dry bones, hear the word of the Lord! This is what the Sovereign Lord says to these bones: I will make breath enter you, and you will come to life. I will attach tendons to you and make flesh come upon you and cover you with skin; I will put breath in you, and you will come to life. Then you will know that I am the Lord." - Ezekiel 37:4-6

God motivates us to speak to our current circumstances and conditions differently than how we feel about our circumstances and opinions of what we see. He tells us to speak words of affirmation, inspiration and rejuvenation to our children, communities and current lifeless relationships and circumstances. He tells us to speak life to those things that had died in the wars and battles of our past. In that same way this is a must for fathers who are incarcerated. Because of obvious reasons, their physical presence is prohibited because of their current circumstances. Their words become vitally important and just as powerful as their physical presence would have been. These are words of affirmation, inspiration and rejuvenation spoken to a society where no one believes that things can be better or can breathe or speak life into dead situations.

5. Ezekiel's willingness to comply to what God asked him to do resulted in him seeing what was hopeless transform to hopefulness. God says optimism to a hopeless situation is always better than pessimism; its results always contradict hopelessness.

So, I prophesied as I was commanded. And as I was prophesying, there was a noise, a rattling sound, and the bones came together, bone to bone. I looked, and tendons and flesh appeared on them and skin covered them, but there was no breath in them."- Ezekiel 37:7-8

The story goes on to say that these bones were very dried, a sign that these individuals were dead for a very long time. So, God told Ezekiel to speak to the dried bones. Communication goes a long way, and affirmation is a powerful tool that forms a life-giving dialog; it is essentially the pathway to solutions. The wrong words can cause death, both figuratively and literally. Our words shouldn't be just thought of as a lot of noise or empty chatter. Words were created by God, a gift from Him that has the power to create and recreate or to do the complete opposite. When Ezekiel spoke to those bones as God instructed him, it didn't matter how long they were dead; tendons began to attach bone to bone, flesh (muscle & fat) began to cover the bone, and skin covered it all.

Afterwards, he instructed Ezekiel to speak to the wind and call for the breath of life to enter into those bodies that they may live. When we walk among our youth and communicate with them, things will begin to come together. When we as men cleave to fatherhood as much as we do our social, political and religious agendas, only then will we secure a future for our children and our communities. Yes, there is hope, but that hope only comes in the form of communication, dialog and listening. If we expect our children to become successful, if we want our communities to thrive, and if our children are to become a force to reckon with, we must speak words that give life. Then and only then will we and our children become great warriors of life.

Then He said to me, 'Prophesy to the wind; prophesy, son of man, and say to the wind: Thus, says the Lord God: Come from the four winds, O breath, and breathe upon these slain so that they live.'

So, I prophesied as he commanded me, and the breath came into them, and they lived, and stood up upon their feet, an exceeding great army. - Ezekiel 37:9-10

Being a father is more than a natural thing; it is a spiritual thing, and when viewed in that context, the importance of fatherhood serves a higher and deeper purpose than our natural and monetary duties. When fathers implement the Ezekiel Effect, the belief in the power of affirmation, inspiration and rejuvenation will change a hopeless situation into a hopeful one. Three things will happen in the parent-child relationship that took place in Ezekiel's vision:

a) They came to life. The living God commanded a living person to speak to dead circumstances and situations. You have to first be revived as a person before you can revive your conditions and circumstances.

b) They stood up. Many people are living, but not empowered. They have emotionally, mentally and spiritually given away the power of their life. Just because you are incarcerated doesn't mean that you have to give away your power to become better. Your situation doesn't forbid you from greatness. Your imprisonment doesn't prohibit your empowerment, so stand up!

c) They were ready for war. You have now readied yourself for the challenges of fatherhood when you do these things.

As an incarcerated father, it may seem impossible to pursue fatherhood from your perspective and valley of disparity, full of dead hopes, aspirations and relationships. Your valley would be the lowest condition and circumstance that you would have never thought you would find yourself. When incarcerated fathers apply the Ezekiel Effect to the lifeless relationship between them and their child, their words will resuscitate that relationship. Then the incarcerated father will begin to see things starting to come together, and that which was once dead will be restored to life while still in his valley.

Let your words touch your children and resound in their hearts from death row, from maximum security and from the great depths and distances, boosting their ambitions for a better life. Talk to your children as though your words may be your last. You can accomplish this by writing letters, through phone calls, or reading bedtime stories, or just talking about life and giving fatherly advice to them via audio or video devices. Use these things as vehicles to transport your words to your children. They will be a valuable tangible part of you that you will leave behind.

Your children will share your words with their children and their children's children. Words can put together that which had been broken and heal the scars that your absence may have caused. They can make amends for the things that ultimately took you out of their lives through your vigorous efforts to reconnect with them. Your words to your children will indirectly help lift some of the heavy burdens from the shoulders of their mother as well. There is no walls, cells, bars, nor restraints that can detain the power of your words.

Every prison across this country should develop a program focused on getting incarcerated fathers back into the lives of their children. This type of program would make a significant difference in the prison community. Heck, even the warden and the correctional officers who may be fathers would benefit from such a program. There are well over 1.1 million incarcerated fathers in this country, impacting an estimated over 2.5 million children's lives. That means that incarcerated fathers have the potential to be 1.1 million strong in having a positive influence on 2.5 million children. Incarcerated fathers can start a fatherhood coalition or support group, discussing issues that they face as imprisoned fathers and coming up with creative ideas and solutions to the problems that their children will face as children of an incarcerated father. Developing a newsletter for incarcerated fathers and distributing it to inmates, employees and visitors would be a great idea. Ideas like these can produce positive results, impacting greatly the lives of any and every one that steps in or out of the prison walls.

The call to fatherhood behind prison walls will encourage fathers of every ethnic, religious and social persuasion to come together for one common cause. When men begin to talk about the hopes and dreams that they have for their sons and daughters, it will break all barriers. Even bigotry takes a backseat when fathers start talking about the hopes, dreams and accomplishments of and for their children.

If incarcerated fathers refuse to be involved in their children's lives, if they refuse to pursue fatherhood, they will have sentenced themselves to life never knowing the joy of being a father. Fathers who are incarcerated become successful at fatherhood when they break free from the barriers of the guilt of the past, and when the only reason their children will ever step foot in prison is when they come to visit them.

Chapter 13:

FATHER, WHY HAVE THOU

FORSAKEN ME?

To forsake is to abandon or withdraw companionship, affection, protection, to deny availability to or refuse support from someone.[2] When a father abandons a child, it retards them; it delays and holds them back. Their progress for developing emotionally, mentally and spiritually will often slow future accomplishments or, at worst, completely prevent them from achieving future success unless that child has a father figure or the support of an endearing loving mother, as is often the case. Women have always had to step up when men stepped down from their roles as fathers.

A parent's abandonment or even the feeling of being abandoned by a parent is the worst thing a child can experience. It is the same as rejection and synonymous with not being loved. It leaves a child wondering why, with no answers given nor none to be found.

Abandonment does not only come in the form of a deadbeat or uninvolved father, but it can come in the form of

---

[2] Merriam-Webster's Collegiate Dictionary, 1999

a generous father with a good job. Some fathers become so engulfed in and committed to their careers that they omit the responsibility of being involved with their children (As in the case of the story of the Prodigal Son). Usually, when a father abandons a child, that child will choose and replace that void with fake unsavory companionship and affection of unscrupulous friendship. They will misconstrue what is artificial for real and genuine love and fellowship. They will replace right for wrong, looking for love in gangs, pimps, drug dealers, sugar daddies and sugar mommas, sex, etc. Children will do this consciously or subconsciously, all in the attempt to replace the one who abandoned them.

Because of poor self-esteem, a young woman may become more accepting of the battering from an abusive man. Subconsciously, the abuse is worth taking to keep her false sense of security that he provides. Children will gravitate to people who give them a false sense of protection, companionship, and support, eventually leaving them with no hope, peace, self-worth, and, ultimately, no life.

While some substitutions are not necessarily harmful, they are only substitutions. Artificial plants are beautiful and can bring beauty to a room, but they do not possess the same qualities of a real plant which removes dangerous toxins from the air, making healthier air to breathe, bringing a fresh aroma to the room. As a non-residential father, we must keep our children away from things or people that can be toxic to their lives, but only if we're there and involved can this be accomplished. Real things have substance and life-changing benefits; artificial things only look the part, but have no real benefits or potential for growth, only having the perception of being real. Fake things are substandard to real things.

When we substitute artificial stuff in place of real things, it will only provide our children with illusions for real life. Many of our youth have accepted illusions in place of what is real, only because the real thing was not available to them. So, we as fathers must be available to our children at any cost, or our children will pay a high price for accepting an illusion. In the words of the great Marvin Gaye and Tammi Terrell, "Ain't Nothing Like the Real Thing Baby."

Fathers must be present to show children what is real and what is not real; we must give them the benefits that only our authenticity provides. Then and only then will they be able to discern the fake from what is real and avoid the wolves in sheep's clothing.

Even doing those things we deem necessary, socially noble and acceptable becomes unacceptable if we place them over our children's wellbeing, and when it prevents us from being nurturing parents. Having a job, career, business or being a minister, motivational speaker, block captain, politician, even the President of the United States, are all socially acceptable and noble pursuits. But if these socially acceptable worthy pursuits hinder a man from being actively involved in his children's lives, then that man's priorities are in the wrong place, and his pursuits become socially unacceptable and not noble. His pursuit is misguided, and he is guilty of child abandonment.

The most devastating thing to a child is not so much the separation of a mother and father, but rather the fear that their father might no longer be a loving part of their life. The child may rationalize that he (the father) left mom because he didn't love her anymore; maybe he doesn't love me either. A child will take on the daunting task of doing things in hopes that the father will continue to love them. Children all over the world are feeling the effects of fatherlessness; they feel forsaken and inwardly are crying out, Father, why have you forsaken me? What have I done to deserve this? How can I fix this? In their attempts to find the answers to these questions, they are often left with no explanation and begin to display socially unacceptable behaviors.

Fathers may not fully realize the powerful effects that their mere presence has on their children. It's amazing how a simple phone call from Dad can uplift a child. Even something as small as asking, how was your day? How was school? Did you do your homework? How was work? What's wrong? Or Do you need anything? And just calling to say goodnight, is just as powerful as you being there reading them a bedtime story, tucking them in and kissing them on their forehead before bed. These simple interactions will make them feel loved. It's incredible how just the mere act of a father walking into a room can affect a child.

Even if all hell breaks loose, and the foundation under your feet begins to crumble, if you lose your job and life beats you down, don't forsake your children. Your presence is vital to their spiritual, emotional, mental and physical survival. The things you say and do will help shape and mold your children; it will set the course for your children's future.

In an article entitled 'Fathers Make a Difference' prepared by Dr. Wayne Matthews, Ph.D., Human Development Specialist, North Carolina Cooperative Extension Service, suggestions of how fathers who don't live with their children can stay connected with them are as follows:

•*Parenting in the same ways he did before the divorce.*

•*Providing childcare while mom works.*

•*Transporting children to and from school or social and sporting events.*

•*Providing daily childcare.*

•*Spending a week or weekend in the child's hometown rather than always having the child travel.*

•*Using e-mail, phone, videos and photographs to stay in touch. Web-cams allow online conversations with live video.*

No child should ever have to ask the question, *Daddy, why have you forsaken me?*

Chapter 14:

DIAMONDS IN THE ROUGH

There should be no cause or reason for a father to forsake a child. Not even a child's disability should disqualify him or her from receiving the love and attention of a father. In this chapter, I bring my views on a topic rarely discuss when talking about fatherhood, and that is fathers of special-needs children. Every parent wishes that their child would be born healthy, mentally, physically and emotionally. Unfortunately, this is not always the case.

Parents who have taken on the challenging task of raising a child with special needs deserve much praise. Yet, no parent should be judged negatively for deciding to place a special need child in a facility that serves the unique needs of individuals who benefit from and can be bettered care for and receive direct care and help with their challenges. I have not had to raise a child who has special mental or physical needs, so I won't pretend to know the difficulties of doing so. But what I can say is that if a father turns away from this most challenging, yet rewarding opportunity, that father is a coward and denies himself.

Some fathers are unwilling to accept this challenge, reluctant to step up to the plate of fatherhood. They will leave this challenging task to the mother or a family member. But true men will embrace this challenge and stay faithful to the call of fatherhood despite a child's disability. Fathers of children who has special needs should see these precious children like any other children_as gifts from God needing the loving attention of a parent. Fathers should help the special need child see the possibilities, reach goals, and dig deep into untapped potentials by not focusing on what that child cannot do, but instead, they should focus on what they can do. Every child with special deserves the unyielding support and affection of a mother and father as it is crucial to their development. If we look at it, every child has their individual special needs, even those diagnosed as normal.

Facilities that care for special-needs children should require parents to play an active role in their children's development and progress. Part of their funding should be allocated for that purpose. Programs that focus on parent-outreach and encourage parental involvement are needed. Parents of special-needs children must keep in mind that these facilities are not meant to take the place of a loving, involved father or mother. These facilities should be used only as augmenting services to parenting.

I commend those fathers who are raising special-needs children and have committed themselves to make sure they receive the happy and healthy life that they deserve. If you are a father of special-needs child or children, I hope that you stay active and nurturing; never stop seeing the possibilities that they possess. These children are diamonds in the rough, and while their appearance and actions may be underestimated, their potential should not. The things that they are unable to do often cast a shadow over the things they can do. Every child deserves a father, especially the special-needs child. Here's a list of a few famous people who have or had disabilities:

Tom Wiggins- African American pianist who was legally blind and autistic (a mental condition, present from early childhood, characterized by difficulty in communicating and forming relationships with other people).

Albert Einstein- Famous physicist who had Asperger's Syndrome, a developmental disorder related to autism and characterized by higher than average intellectual ability coupled with impaired social skills and restrictive, repetitive patterns of interest and activities, and autism.

Thomas Edison- An American inventor who had ADHD, a disorder in which a person is unable to control behavior due to difficulty in processing neural stimuli, accompanied by an extremely high level of motor activity. He also was dyslexic, which involved a disorder concerning difficulty in learning to read or interpret words, letters and other symbols, but did not affect general intelligence.

James Earl Jones- African American actor who had a speech impairment and stuttered.

Wolfgang Amadeus Mozart- Renowned composer who had Tourette syndrome (a neurological disorder characterized by repetitive, stereotyped, involuntary movements and vocalizations called tics).

Wilma Rudolph- First African American woman to win three gold medals in one Olympic game, and had polio, a condition that causes paralysis, difficulty breathing and sometimes death.

Harriet Tubman- Anti-Slavery Activist & Women Suffragist suffered from epilepsy, a neurological disorder marked by sudden recurrent episodes of sensory disturbance, loss of consciousness or convulsions, associated with abnormal electrical activity in the brain.

Helen Keller- Educator/Activist, was deaf and blind.

Woodrow Wilson- President of the United States of America who had dyslexia.

Vincent van Gogh- Famous Dutch artist who had bipolar disorder. Bipolar disorder, formerly called manic depression, causes extreme mood swings that include emotional highs called mania or hypomania, and lows known as depression.

Stevie Wonder- Renowned musician and songwriter is blind.

Tom Cruise- Actor and filmmaker who is dyslexic.

Danny Glover- An American actor, film director and political activist. The school system labeled him retarded when he in fact was dyslexic.

General George Patton- United States Army general who is dyslexic.

Whoopi Goldberg- An American actress, comedian, writer, social critic and television host who is also dyslexic.

Sylvia Walker- Former Director of The Center for Disability and Socioeconomic Policy Studies at the Howard University Research and Training Center who was also blind.

What is most ironic is that these individuals have or had disabilities that should have prevented them from being successful and excelling in their chosen professions, but that was not the case. Despite their disability and against all the odds, their will proved more potent than the opposing forces they embodied. They and so many like them are living proof that a person's disability does not disable them from success; they only find a different path to it.

Chapter 15:

THE "R" WORD

It is much too late for any male, young or old, to begin considering whether or not they want to be a father after they've played a part in bringing a child into the world. And I would not tell a woman what she should do with her body, as far as pro-life or pro-choice is concerned, despite my personal beliefs. But I will say this: it is not about a woman's right to do what she wants to do with her body or a man's right to have sexual relationships with any woman with whom he chooses. That is an argument that the religious and the non-religious world will continue to debate for years to come. I will reserve getting into my personal religious or political opinion about this topic because that's not the focus of this book. But what I will say is that there is only one answer to this topic, and that is RESPONSIBILITY.

We must be responsible stewards of the choices we make, realizing that consequence follows irresponsibility. As fathers, we must be accountable for our mistakes and poor decisions, and we must convey this to our children as well. By taking ownership of our mistakes and poor choices, we show responsibility at its highest level for our lowest times in life. As fathers, we must be proactive in dealing with the consequences of our mistakes and poor choices, admonishing our children to do the same, teaching them that mistakes don't have to be an end-all thing; it is when we fail to learn from them that it ends all. Teaching children how to deal with mistakes and poor decisions is a parent's responsibility, and failing to do so is a mistake and a poor decision on that parent's part.

We sometimes allow our human cravings to take priority over the responsible thing to do. Responsibility is the obligation of every human being. We are irresponsible when we, as adults, do not take responsibility for what we do with our bodies. We sometimes take more responsibility for material things (i.e., cars, homes, jewelry and jobs) than we do our bodies and unfortunately, at times than we do our children. We make sure we have insurance policies and warranties. We lock things in safe boxes that we consider precious, not even wanting people to touch them, fearing that they may smudge or damage. Yet, we remain reckless and irresponsible with our bodies.

Irresponsibility ultimately causes the decay of our self-worth and self-esteem, chipping away at us spiritually, emotionally and mentally, ultimately affecting our communities. If we're not careful, we can transfer these same destructive, irresponsible behaviors to our posterity. Men and women, husbands and wives, fathers and mothers, must regain a sense of responsibility and must teach responsibility to their children. When we become responsible, we save ourselves from an abundance of hurt and agony. When we become responsible as non-residential fathers, we keep our children from similar pains and sufferings, as shown in the statistics cited earlier from the National Fatherhood Initiative and the U.S. Department of Justice. It doesn't mean that we as fathers are going to be perfect, but we can no longer afford to allow self-indulgence to keep us from the pursuit of fatherhood. We must become responsible for the consequences of our irresponsibility.

Chapter 16:

REAL TALK

REAL TALK is about keeping it real, genuine and saying the things people don't want to say. It's about expressing sincere thoughts and opinions; facing facts and not sugarcoating our life experiences, good or bad. It's about speaking the truth regarding those things that only prove that; indeed, we are human.

Real Talk #1

As parents, we must make sure that our children are not living as latchkey kids. I know that your jobs, church, and yes, even your social life and status is important to you. However, our children are more important than those things or any other thing that we as parents consider of value. From the moment they emerge from the womb, our children becomes our number one priority in life. That being said, our children should not come home to an empty house or be left to themselves day in and day out, hours upon hours, especially in those pre-teen and adolescent ages. This is the time when natural inquisitiveness starts to come into play. Parents need to be around in these times of burning curiosity to educate and guide their children through their feelings, desires, thoughts and emotions. Curiosity is not a bad thing; it only says that our children are human, and it opens an opportunity for teachable moments. It is a natural phenomenon, but when this natural phenomenon goes unchecked, it leads to making unwise and destructive choices. We need only to remember what curiosity did to the cat. Look where curiosity got Adam and Eve; man and woman have been paying a heavy price for their curiosity ever since. This situation requires both parents' involvement.

Every responsible father and parent should ensure that idle time does not dominate their children's lives and that their children are in a nurturing environment.

Real Talk # 2

Some non-residential fathers may disagree with what I'm about to say, but here goes. The non-residential father should do whatever he can to make sure the mother of his children does not become mentally or emotionally taxed by the stresses of life, which can significantly affect their children's well-being. For example, if that mother finds herself laid off and is struggling to make ends meet, keeping utilities on and the child is living with her, then the non-residential father should not stand by idly and say: "That's what she gets; now we'll see who's the better parent."

In instances such as this, if the mother is not involved in another relationship (or maybe if she is), a non-residential father should offer whatever aid that will help relieve this stress of the mother and for the child's sake. When children live with their mother, her mental, emotional and spiritual well-being is necessary for the child's growth and well-being, and vice versa. This is not an emotional attachment to that mother or father, but rather an obligation to their child's welfare. We must learn to make concessions as parents for the sake of our kids. This is being true to the call of parenthood. It is the right direction in the pursuit of fatherhood. When divorced parents see that their child/children are facing difficult times, they should come together, put all their differences aside and become allies for a common goal_ the nurturing and safety of their children. It is the right thing to do. Nothing about that child should be held in secret from the other parent, with some few exceptions.

Real Talk #3

Non-residential fathers must be careful when they become involved in new relationships (mothers as well). If the woman that you are involved with cannot understand your commitment to your children or want you to choose between your children and them, then you should close the door on that relationship. People who get involved in a relationship where one person in that relationship has a child should realize that it is like buying a car with a sign that says "sold as is," as such, they must be willing to take on whatever comes with that person.

Also, as non-residential fathers, we should be very reserved about the women that we bring around our children. Sometimes it is best to delay this until we know who we're fully getting ourselves into.

Real Talk #4

Those who are parents of young school-aged sons, who have gotten a young school-aged girl pregnant, should not delay in the teaching of responsibility to these children. As unfortunate as the situation may be, playing the blame game or continuously pointing or shaking a scolding finger at these children is fruitless. Once is enough, then we must go into proactive mode. These young children have prematurely stepped into the realm of parenthood. It then becomes the responsibility of the parents to teach each child about their roles as parents.

A father should make sure his son knows that the responsibility of raising a child is as important as doing your homework and more important than playing on a school varsity sports team. The father should encourage the son to visit and spend time with that child because this is what real men do. Likewise, a mother should make sure her daughter becomes equally responsible for raising that child, teaching her about motherhood while still allowing her to keep her childhood. No parent wants this situation to happen to their children, but if it does, we must become proactive in this premature circumstance. As unfortunate as this situation may be, we must turn it into a teachable moment. A moral debate for this state of affairs is irrelevant at this point and time. The lives of these young people will drastically change, and as parents, we should help them navigate through this situation that they find themselves in because of their poor choices.

I choose to withhold my personal religious beliefs on sexual promiscuity, but it does not distract me from addressing the proactive role that a father must play in times like these. Sometimes our religious dogmas override our responsibility and the opportunity we're presented with to educate our children while going through these situations.

These hypothetical social situations that I have presented are as real as our religious beliefs. Being proactive in a bad situation is better than not being active at all, or at worse, being active in a way that is more destructive than helpful. We can prevent this type of situation when we as fathers begin to place our children's needs above our own by becoming involved in their lives. But even then, there is always the possibility that something may go wrong.

I believe that we can lower the statistics of children giving birth to children by at least 75-80% when we put parenting before pleasure, jobs, careers and before other people. When we put parenting first, our viewpoints about these issues will take a backseat to what's necessary. Abortion and contraception are not real resolutions to this problem; they can only serve as methods abused by irresponsible people, they become things that are used so parents can shirk their responsibility by not teaching responsibility, self-respect and control. Who would have known that teaching our children self-respect, self-esteem and self-care of their body would come in an edited version, wrapped in a foil or plastic wrapper? Contraceptives have become a way to hide sexual promiscuity rather than a method of prevention. They may prevent the birth of a child, but it doesn't prevent the emotional, mental and spiritual traumas and dramas that come with being promiscuous. Telling a child to make sure they wear a condom or remember to take a birth control pill is not teaching responsibility_we made it that.

Abstinence is a good thing, but our society wants us to believe it's only theoretical. If it was just theory then we wouldn't have virgins in the world. However, good parenting is the need for every child's growth and well-being. Parenting is a reality that's stamped with God's seal of approval.

Real Talk #5

You would probably be surprised by the sacrifices and choices some women have made so that they could take care of their children; sacrifices and choices that to this day whittle away at the integrity of their souls imbalanced with guilt by what they deemed necessary at that time. Things that they did that they will take to their grave with them. Some things that not even their children will ever know. Even though it was done for them, some children may find out what those mothers did some years later after that mother has passed. Some of these choices society would classify as sinful, degrading and shameful. If you would ask these mothers would they do the same thing over again for the sake of their children, their answer would be indubitably, "YES! For my children, yes I would!"

Even with my social and religious viewpoints, I dare not throw a stone at them for the choices and sacrifices these mothers felt they had to make for the sake of their children. For, in doing so, I might be throwing a stone at my mother or grandmother who probably unbeknownst to me, made some of the same sacrifices and choices. Many of these women have done well raising their children, and for the most part, have succeeded in giving them a better life than what they had. These women look into the eyes of their children with no regrets, and wear scars of the sacrifices of their choices like medals of valour. I cast no stones at such women; instead, I would save my stones for those fathers who could have been a much-needed help and reinforcement to that single mother. But instead, these cowards choose to abandon their responsibilities as fathers, not lifting a finger to help raise their children. That stone of judgment I save for them, and just maybe if I aim as straight with it as the stone that David used to slay Goliath, I can hit them right between the eyes and watch the fall of the fatherlessness. That's real talk!

Real Talk #6

We must stop blaming all our nation's problems on the government, politicians, criminals, hate and separatist groups, etc. There are many factors that we face in our society which we can attribute to fatherlessness, essentially fathers not being involved with their children. Might it be because some father's father was never around to help him develop as a man and notice his development of poor self-esteem and destructive behavior, is the reason why he is not sensitive enough to see it in himself? We must not be fathers who instill in their children their own bigotries and hatreds, as well as flaunt immorality around their children in the name of so-called manhood.

Being a good parent isn't about teaching a particular religion or political viewpoint. It's about loving your children enough to let them be their own person and to have their own thoughts and opinions. But you must be around to help guide them through those thoughts and opinions. Fatherhood is about protecting the children whom you were blessed to have, even if that means protecting them from the worst parts of yourself. We, as fathers, should help and encourage our children to grow, develop and thrive at their own pace, in their own way. We must stop trying to live vicariously through them or mold them into who we think they should be. We should encourage them to chase their own dreams and not the dreams we wish they would pursue.

Our role as fathers/parents is to be there for them, and to be a positive, life-giving and inspiring influence in their lives. We must realize that having no influence in their lives is just as bad as being a bad influence. Both have adverse effects.

Real Talk #7

There are good mothers and fathers, and there are bad mothers and fathers. Every good parent deserves the right to be a part of their child's life. Gender should have no bearing on their ability to be a parent. Mothers and fathers should be equally responsible for raising their child/children. Children deserve equal exposure as much as possible from both parents. Unfortunately, our family court system decisions are often gender bias. Sadly, this gender bias has caused some good fathers to relinquish their rights as parents, abandoning the call to fatherhood altogether. Our family court laws must be evaluated, revised and reconstructed. Otherwise, family courts will only continue to aid in the destruction of the father-child relationship.

When disgruntled exes use the system against dedicated and responsible fathers, it's the children that become the casualty. Fathers must not give up the fight or the effort to change the family court system. They should not get so distracted that they spend more time fighting the system and less time with their children. Otherwise, you might find yourself winning the fight on one front, but losing it on the other. I am not a proponent or believer in FCS as it stands.

Real Talk #8

Fathers and mothers must stop handing over their God-given rights as parents into the hands of lawyers and judges. When we do this, we are letting a flawed system, which knows nothing about our children decide what's best for our children. Rather than allowing family courts to dictate our roles as parents, we must be mature adults and work together as parents, making decisions together based on the betterment of the children. To do this, both parents must swallow their pride, stop being vindictive, heal their hurts, and get over it so that they can get on to the important task of parenting void of unnecessary self-inflicted distractions.

Of course, depending on what type of ex you're dealing with and the relationship you have with them, it may be necessary to go through family court. As flawed as it may be, family courts do serve some purpose to that respect. Parenting is not an easy task, but that's why raising children should be a joint effort between mother and father, even if they are no longer joined in holy matrimony. If it took two of you to make that child, it would take both of you to raise them. In the end, it's all about the children.

And that my friend is REAL TALK.

Chapter 17:

MY TWO GOALS

As a non-residential father, my two main goals that I wanted to accomplish were:

1) I wanted my daughters to know who I am. I did not just want to be this person that visited them on occasions. I needed to achieve this through an enduring committed relationship with them. Although I didn't live with them, I made myself available to them as though I did.

2) I wanted to make sure they knew one another. As I mentioned earlier, my three girls are the result of two different relationships; two of my daughters shared the same mother and my youngest daughter has a different mother. I made it my responsibility to make sure that these three beautiful girls grew up with each other, knowing and being around each other as much as possible. I wanted them to know that even though they had different mothers, they were just as much as sisters as I was their father. I did not want my daughters to grow up only knowing *of* each other; I wanted them to grow up *knowing* each other, playing with each other, laughing with each other and sharing good and bad times with each other. This goal took a lot of time and effort on my part; I had to coordinate schedules so I could have all three of them at the same time. I

couldn't have done it without some excellent cooperation and understanding from their mothers. Most times, I was able to accomplish this, but sometimes I was unable to.

I thank God, they know each other and love being around each other. They even ask about each other when they don't see each other for a week or so. When they get together, they fuss and fight for at least 2-3 minutes, as siblings do, but even through those sibling rivalries, I can tell that they love each other. Both older sisters were very protective of their little sister.

Those times were worth everything to me. It makes me happy when I have all three of them at the same time. One time when they were in the car with me they had one of those sibling rivalries; it got on my nerves so bad that I said: "If you guys don't keep quiet, I'm taking each of you back home to your mothers." As they sat quietly, I saw the hurt in their eyes which made me feel the worst that I've ever felt. I apologized to them and since that day, I have made a commitment that no matter how much they get on my nerves (which children will sometimes do), I will never say anything like that to them ever again. They should feel comfortable and free to engage with each other, good or bad, like siblings, without the fear or threat of being separated.

When a man has children from different relationships, it is his responsibility to take care of them. As much as possible, make sure they are actively involved with each other and know each other, not just know *of* each other. This is a task that often will inconvenience you as a father, but it will turn out to be an inconvenience that is worth it.

Chapter 18:

THE ANATOMY OF INVOLVEMENT

Remember reading earlier about the vision of the valley of dry bones that God gave Ezekiel? Likewise, we can compare the role of fatherhood to the body's anatomy parts and their functions. Here are some main anatomical parts that Ezekiel may have seen come together after he spoke to them in his vision of the valley of dry bones.

SKELETAL SYSTEM (The Framework):

Bone, when put together with other bone, form a skeleton. The skeletal system is the framework of the body consisting of bones and other connective tissues; this framework protects and supports the body tissues and internal organs. Moreover, it provides a base for muscles to attach through tendons. It also helps to maintains balance and the body's form. Marrow is found in bone; it makes red and white blood cells. These cells are critical to the body's immune and respiratory systems. All these functions together assist in the stable locomotion of the body. When bones become dry and fragile, they lose their ability to protect vulnerable organs. They lose the capacity to produce and move the blood cells needed to fight off infections and other foreign materials, and to deliver oxygen, nutrients, heat and hormones within the body. In short, the bone provides structure, support and protection for the body.

In like manner, fathers offer structure, support and security for children, a framework by which children can build on. Our active presence protects our children and our nurturing involvement gives them the inner strength to fight off the negative social influences of life. What we instill in our children gives them the ability to fight off the internal and external infections of peer pressure. Our force enables them to maintain a healthy spiritual, emotional and mental posture. This is the power of fatherhood. This framework of bones and connective tissue called the skeleton is evident by the external surface, but is deeply embedded and unseen. Without the skeletal system, the body is a lifeless diseased blob. And so are our children without our involvement in their lives. And so is our community without the participation of fathers.

SINEW (Healthy Attachment):

Sinew is a term used that means tendons or ligaments. A tendon is a fibrous connective tissue which attaches muscle to bone. Tendons may also attach muscles to structures such as the eyeball. A ligament is a fibrous connective tissue which attaches bone to bone, and usually serves to hold structures together and keep them stable.[3]

Much like tendons and ligaments, fathers are the connective tissue of society, community and children. They are uniters; their involvement helps give their children stability. Fathers gives their children a healthy and robust attachment to real life; they become a child's most significant power source. And like tendons that connect muscle to bone, a father's involvement in his children's lives enables them to walk in, run through, jump over and lift whatever society brings their way. When a father is actively involved in his children's lives, those children have the potential to become the movers and shakers of society.

Ligaments connect bone to bone, providing stability at the joints. A father's active involvement in his children's life helps provide mental, emotional and spiritual stability because of his active participation. These tendons and ligaments prevent hyperextension and flexion of a joint as well; in other words, they stop joints from bending too far and prevent them from turning in the wrong direction.

Your active involvement will not create a perfect child, but it will instill in them limits; it will create in them a sense

---

[3] MedlinePlus Medical Encyclopedia, Imagemedlineplus.gov › Medical Encyclopedia, 2018

of social and personal moderation. Your guidance will keep them from mental and emotional hyperextension. Your presence will give them the courage to lean or bend in the right direction. Your influence as fathers will create a sense of stability in them. Your active involvement will provide them with the ability to exercise sound judgment.

MUSCLES (Building Strength):

Muscles are tissues composed of cells or fibers that contract and help move the body. They maintain posture and generate heat. They are also responsible for giving us the power and strength to perform athletic and everyday tasks. In like manner, a father's regularly scheduled involvement with his children helps to build in them a strong identity, empowers their self-esteem and strengthens good character in that child and in the father-child relationship.

When a father is involved, it helps to create the force needed to succeed by allowing them to see how the father navigates through the ups and downs of life, specifically when a child sees their father trying to achieve something, making something successful of himself by building a career or just bettering himself as a man. When they see their father attempting these things and fail, yet amid the failures get back up and try again, they are seeing power and strength in action.

It doesn't matter if that father is successful in those things at that particular time. It is how that father handles disappointment, failure and setbacks; this is the most inspiring to a child. The dedication and perseverance to succeed is transferred to that child. A father's involvement breeds confidence in children, causing them to stand erect with confidence in their abilities, even amid their inabilities. They will be strong enough to react positively under the weight of peer pressure.

This world is often cold and unforgiving; our children need the power and strength to overcome its rigidness. Because they are around to see your strength in action, they will inherit the ability to exhibit the same strength themselves.

Honorable fathers are those who instill in their children the ability to distinguish between right and wrong and the difference between good behavior and bad behavior. They can exercise the strength to choose right over wrong and good behavior over bad. We must show them through our actions that people of bravery, integrity and strength are those who choose right over wrong and good behavior over bad, while weak and cowardly people don't, no matter how strong they may appear to be.

FAT (Human Emotions):

Fat is a kind of body tissue that serves as a source of energy; it cushions and insulates vital organs, creating warmth. A father must display the ability to comfort, show fatherly affection, and should not be afraid to display genuine human emotions, such as regularly and appropriately hugging and kissing their sons and daughters.

Fat also regulates temperature, nutrients and maintains healthy skin, hair and nails. Fathers teach children to control their emotions. Even the greatest man in history, Jesus, wasn't afraid to show His emotions as the scripture says:

Jesus wept. -John 11:35

Some have speculated why Jesus displayed such emotion; whatever the case may be, Jesus was so heartbroken that He cried. One of the greatest thing for a child to see is that their father is human and is not some god-like figure. It is something magical to a child when they see their father displays warmth in times when comfort is needed.

SKIN (Wrap-Around):

The skin is our outer lay that wraps around all internal system, it protects us from microbes and external elements. In fact, the skin is the body's largest organ. The role of fathers/men is to safeguard their children from outside social external elements and bacteria; form societal disease that corrupts the mind, spirit, and soul. Whatever you put on your skin or whatever your skin is exposed to will absorb into the body. We especially must be protective of our children at an early age, making sure that not only their physical, but their mental and spiritual being is not exposed to toxic people or things. We must wrap ourselves completely around our children, especially in those formative years, being mindful that whatever we absorb into our lives will affect them. Those are the years that we must take exceptional care of the kind of environment we build around them. And the environment we create around them, the people we expose them to will be absorbed by them. Like a security blanket, parents should wrap themselves securely and protectively around their children.

OXYGEN (Breath of Life):

Oxygen/breath is not an anatomical body part, but it is the life source for every organ of the body; in every living person, animal and plant life. Without this essential phenomenon, none of the anatomical parts described will function. If there is no oxygen, there is no life. And so it is with the father/child relationship.

When a child is born, they are empty vessels waiting to be filled. From the time of birth well into the age of adolescence, what we breathe in them will determine the success of their adulthood. Parents have the unique responsibility to supply their children with that which will bring life.

Every child has what it takes to become somebody, to live to their full potential. They already have what is needed to become successful in life; they need only inspiration and someone to inspire them to action. They need a father to nurture that potential, and encourage them; they need a father that will breathe life to that which is already in them. A father's loving instructions to his children are the breath that gives life to them. The instructions that we give our kids and the manner in which we give them instruction, the things we say to them, and the things they see and hear will shape their thoughts and be displayed in their actions.

Part of breathing is inhaling, which is referred to as inspiration. What is it that's in our social atmosphere that our children are inhaling into their minds and spirits? What are they taking in? Is the environment clean or is it polluted? Is the atmosphere that we create toxins in them, or is it an atmosphere that stimulates them to success and morality? Do we stimulate their inner creativity, good ideas and dreams? Or are we allowing our children to inhale the pollutions of society, and the toxic and malignant influence of negative people? Worst yet, are they inhaling polluted, toxic, cancerous ways, thoughts, and actions we have as parents?

When God created man, the man was just a lifeless body with no ability, inspiration, motion or life, yet with amazing potential. God breathed life into man's body, and man became a living soul; his potential was maximized, and he was alive

123

ready to rule the world. As fathers, we have this same type of power, the power to breathe life into our children, making them successful rulers of their destiny. We also possess the means to destroy our children's lives, potentially leaving lifeless souls lying to decay like food for vultures. For which will we choose to be responsible?

Unfortunately, many of our youth today are like zombies, much like the walking dead, polluted with the toxins of our society. Not only are they toxic, but they are infectious, spreading lethal toxins to and with whomever they come in contact. They have no inspiration for life. And just like the walking dead, they serve no purpose other than to wreak havoc on those who are alive. They leave behind a lifeless society, deprived communities and a bleak and hopeless future. Without a father's guidance and involvement, they are all doomed to utter destruction.

Not only do our children need a father's involvement, but our communities do as well. As we look around, we see our youth wasting time. We see the rise of crime committed by our youth, our prisons overflowing with our youth, and most of all, we see our youth killing one another. As adults, we fail our youth because we abandon the role of being fathers and mothers of the community. We look out into our communities, and we see lifelessness, hopelessness and destruction. Hope seems to elude us. But all is not lost, and we can rediscover hope; when we as parents, especially fathers, become actively involved in the lives of our children and our communities and begin breathing life into them once again.

Young people who commit crimes and those who allow themselves to become victims (because of low self-esteem) share one thing in common: that is the absence of a loving father that can breathe life into them.

Chapter 19:
FATHER EXCHANGE STUDENT
PROGRAM
(An Impact on My Personal Life)

It is difficult raising children in a dysfunctional home, though raising children is not an easy task, even in a functional family setting. Some parents find it more difficult than other parents raising children partly because they were not raised in a home saturated with the love and care of involved parents. They are not sure of or have a blueprint of what it is like, so they wing it. When a parent is unable or unwilling to show love to their children, it is a sign that that parent's soul has been broken. Often parents deprived of love will deprive their children of love, and their children will develop the mental, emotional and spiritual incapacity to parent successfully. Often this is not a direct fault of the parent, but an indirect residual effect of something that happened to them in the past, usually way before they had children or when their children were too young to remember.

Sometimes a parent's inability to raise their children could stem from a mental or emotional breakdown brought on by physical abuse, alcohol and drug use or by being raised in a dysfunctional household. I consider myself one that was raised in a somewhat (maybe not somewhat) dysfunctional home. I was informally in a program that had a similar name as the title of this chapter: Exchange Student Program for Children. My involvement in this "program" came more out of necessity, it happened in a more organic way and not because such a program ever existed. Let me tell you a story. It's a story about me in my teens and a man and his wonderful family. A family that took me in as their own and had a lasting positive influence on my life as a man and later, as a father.

In an earlier chapter, I shared the emotional and mental problems from which my mother suffered. I had my own issues as well, with stored up anger in my soul and stockpiles of unforgiveness. Even though at a glance, I appeared to be a healthy, well-balanced child, I was not. I welcomed the opportunity for someone, anyone to push my button. I was like an active volcano inside. Every day I was erupting internally, anger and resentment ready to gush out like hot lava from an angry volcano, ready to devour everything in its path. Fear and uncertainty filled my environment like the ashes from a volcano blackening the sky; they were as the infirmities from my weak self-esteem, blocking out the light of hope from entering my soul.

These unresolved emotions in me, compounded by the mental and emotional instability of my mom, caused me and her to clash at times. One of those clashes resulted in me running away from home at about 1:30ish in the morning. I walked hopelessly through the night, only to end up at the doorstep of the assistant pastor of the church I attended at that time. This was someone I looked up to as a father figure and mentor. I banged and banged and banged on the door until I saw lights illuminating inside the home. Pastor Floyd Wheeler opened the door and invited me in, and said, "It's Ray," informing his wife Nancy who it was as she stood at the top of the stairway. As I stood in the middle of his living room floor, Pastor Floyd asked me several times why I was out and knocking on his door at that hour. I stood there stubbornly and silent with no reply, filled with anger. He then began to make it clear to me that I was not going to knock on his door at two o'clock in the morning, and wake him and his family up, only to stand in the middle of his living room with my arms crossed, ignoring him.

Needless to say, after a little tough love, and something having to do with a wooden stick, I felt it in my best interest to answer his questions. After a long conversation, he called my mother to let her know where I was and that I was safe. He also asked would it be ok for me to stay with them for a while; surprisingly with no reluctance, my mom said it was ok. That day sparked the beginning of me living with the Wheeler family for several years. In those years, I saw up-close and firsthand what fatherhood was. In those years, I got a sense of what it felt like to be a father. In those years, I saw this man go through the ups and downs of being a husband and father while having the support of a strong woman at his side. In those years, I was given a chance to experience something I'd never experienced in my life; I finally knew how it felt to have a father in my life.

I watched this man balance fatherhood, work, ministry and being a husband with graceful nimbleness. I watched him navigate through his imperfections and uncertainties while at the same time being strong and confident as a man, husband and father. I saw him angry, sad, disappointed and confused; I witnessed his imperfections, and yes, I even saw him cry; but even then, I never saw anything less than a man. What I saw in him, I used as a compass to guide me through my journey of fatherhood and manhood. He was my Ezekiel, as I watched and studied how he walked through his valley of dry bones. He inspired me to live, saw potential in my life, breathed and spoke life into my lifeless state; he motivated me and caused me to get up from my state of self-pity. And I soon became a man; though flawed, I was stronger than that frail teen that came knocking on his doors in years past.

Fathers and mothers, men and women can do the same thing for some troubled youth as the Wheelers did for me. You can take some disadvantaged young boy or girl into your life and home as an "exchange child/student." Every child who doesn't have a father figure in their life can benefit from such a program. They don't necessarily have to live with you for years as I did with the Wheelers, but you can be a mentor to them. You can invite them over for dinner once a week or spend some weekends with them. If you don't have a child, find someone to whom you can be a parent. Not only would this exchange program benefit the child, but also the parent(s) of that child as well. It will give them some necessary "me time" to that parent who desperately needs it, making them stronger for parenting. For parents who suffer from the emotional, mental, spiritual or financial devastations of life, it will give them space to deal with those things.

When parents become mentors of disadvantaged children, they will begin to see a difference in their community while at the same time, giving some child a fair shake in life. This is one way to help children gain leverage in life, leverage that he or she could never obtain otherwise. It is one of many ways that a village helps to raise a child. A child must see what a father looks like, how a father lives, how he disciplines, how he interacts and how he responds to life challenges. More importantly, that child needs to feel a father's love. Seeing these things are an essential part of the nurturing of a child, even though that father may not be the natural father of that child.

Seeing a father in action is an irreplaceable experience. Their voice, their looks, and the thing they say and do, the expressions on their faces, their distinctive smell, and their love, how they made you feel, and other endearing things can never be forgotten. Instead of talking about how bad troubled kids are, let's try taking in and mentoring these troubled kids, if that's not too much trouble. Fatherhood should not be exclusive; it is and should be inclusive.

Chapter 20:

I DIDN'T LEAVE, I'M JUST NOT THERE

There are two exceptions to the standard definition of a non-residential father, and I've touched on them earlier. These exceptions are fathers who do not live with their children for reasons other than divorce, separation or plain old abandonment. I refer to them as:

1. Occupational non-residential fathers are fathers who have jobs that require them to be away from home for extended periods.

2. Foreign non-residential fathers are fathers who left their country and came to the U.S.A. to secure a better life for their families, but unfortunately could not bring their children and wife with them. Though that father has not abandoned his child/children, the decision to live apart from them can bring the same feelings of guilt and regret. It can produce the same negative statistics as a deadbeat dad if they don't develop creative ways to stay involved. These brave and noble fathers have chosen to make the painstaking decision to leave their families to come to America because of all the civil unrest in their country and work hard to bring their children, wives or close relatives over later. Sometimes, this can take years to happen. If you are one of those fathers, you should not allow

your geographical separation to separate you from your children.

Fathers who fall under these two categories are forced to use a bit more creativity to maintain and develop their relationship with their children. Technology can become a useful tool in both these situations. Tools like social media (Facebook and Twitter, etc.), communicating by using your smartphone verbally, texting, face timing and emailing are great methods of communication. You can also use your home computer or laptop to do the similar thing. Technology has expanded our ability to communicate with these many options of communication. It is good that we are able today to reach out and touch our children from almost any distance, from virtually any place on the globe.

Chapter 21:

INVOLVEMENT MAKES YOU A BETTER FATHER

Some fathers have said to me that they have had a tough time overcoming their drug addictions, but when their children were born, they were able to stop using. Some fathers went to rehab to get help with their addictions because when they saw their child, they knew they had to change. As a father, there has to be a cause that's greater than yourself that causes you to want to change.

When I was a boy of fourteen, my father was so ignorant I could hardly stand to have the old man around. But when I got to be twenty-one, I was astonished at how much he had learned in seven years. -Mark Twain

When you get involved in your children's lives, it will not only change them, but it will change you. We must be willing to forsake what we are comfortable with being. I have found out how much children can change and mature us. Children give you wisdom and growth as a man that you could have never gotten if you had not had them. Yes, there are certain levels that a man will never reach until he has a child or two.

The Electronic Data Information Source (EDIS) at the University of Florida has some helpful information that will help make your involvement in your child's life better. You can find out some information by logging on their EDIS websites: http://www.edis.ifas.ufl.edu/he139 www.edis.ifas.ufl.edu/topics/families/children.html.

1. Make a schedule to visit with your child. Be sure you have regular contact. If possible, try to make a custody arrangement that involves frequent overnight visits with your child. Plan phone calls and visits at regular times so that your child knows what to expect and can look forward to seeing you. Make your schedule one you can live up to. It's great to visit with your child at other times too, but keep this basic schedule as the bare minimum. Remember that what adults call a schedule children call a promise, especially when they expect to get to visit their father after not seeing him for some time.

2. Learn your child's day-to-day routine. Knowing your child's schedule, such as sports events or lessons and arranging your time with them around those events, will help you understand your child's daily life and bring a helpful routine to your time with your child. Find out your child's bedtime, activities and mealtimes. Learn what he or she likes to eat and when he or she likes to eat it. Know what time your child typically does homework and when he or she likes to go out and play.

3. Show interest in your child's school and other activities. Let your child know that the things he or she does when not with you are important to you. Keep up with your child's progress in school, homework assignments and other school-related activities. Speak to your child often about his or her extracurricular activities, fun trips with friends and feelings about school. These conversations show your child that you care about his or her education and want to be a part of all aspects of his or her life.

4. Pay child support. Making these payments is one of the most important things you can do to show your commitment to your child. Few women make enough to house, clothe, feed and educate themselves and their children. You may have a judge tell you to pay child support. It's the law in most places, even if the parents were never married, never lived together and had no prolonged relationship. While making your child support payments, you are showing your child that you care by providing for her or his needs. Also, making these payments will eliminate the most common source of conflict between a mother and father who have separated.

5. Minimize conflict between you and your child's mother. Often there are hard feelings between a mother and a father after separation or divorce. It's important to stop these feelings from spilling over to your relationship with your child. The more you work to reduce conflict with your child's mother, the easier it will be to play an important, healthy role in your child's life. You will find it's easier to do this if you keep your focus on the well-being of your child.

6. Coordinate parenting strategies with your child's mother. *When a child spends time in two separate homes, differences in parenting styles can be highlighted. In these situations, mothers and fathers may take vastly different approaches to discipline, rewards for the child, and expectations for chores and other responsibilities. Such inconsistencies often leave a child confused and vulnerable to developing a behavioral or emotional problem. It is important to keep a healthy line of communication open with your child's mother regarding parenting practices, expectations for behavior, and other issues related to your child. Try to coordinate these efforts as best you can so that there is true consistency in the homes where your child is raised.*

7. Help your child adjust to other adults who may come into his or her home life. *As time goes by, you and your former spouse will probably become involved in new relationships. This means that your child will probably have other adults come into his or her life. In families who adjust well to life after parental separation, parents recognize the importance of these new adults in their child's life and work to reduce family conflict. At the same time, it is best not to place this other person in a parental or authoritative role over your child right away. Rather, provide opportunities for new adults to get to know and be a friend to your child. These transitions may be difficult for you and your child's mother. Feelings of jealousy, insecurity and outright disapproval are* common. *Try to limit any conflict these feelings may cause between you and your child's mother.*

8. Read to your young child. *Reading to your young child allows you to spend quiet time together one-on-one. It helps to enhance your bond and communication. Also, it demonstrates the high value you place on the role of learning and education in your child's life. It seems so simple, yet it's one of the most important activities that you can do with your child.*

9. Don't be a "vacation" for your child. *Non-residential fathers can sometimes get caught in the trap of always entertaining their child during the brief periods they spend with them. Weekend visits can be filled with trips to amusement parks, the zoo, movies, sporting events, and the like. This can cause several major problems. First, it sets the expectation that something terrific will happen every time the child goes to "daddy's house." These expectations can be both expensive and exhausting. Another problem is that it can make life difficult for the child's mother. If your child spends time with you doing wonderful, exciting things, only to go home to face doing homework, cleaning up their room, or just hanging around the house, the transition back to the mother's home can be difficult. Finally, hectic vacation-like weekends don't allow you to participate in simple, everyday activities with your child like eating meals together, watching a favorite TV show, and taking a bike ride to the park.*

10. Tell your child how much you love them; tell them sincerely and often that you love them. *Children of parents who* *have separated often need extra reassurance that their parents care for them and love them. When you show children love, you reassure them. By communicating your affection, you help your child build a sense of security in her or his life. Non-residential fathers are important sources of advice and emotional support. Children need to know that you will be there to help them with their struggles.*

Enjoy your transformation.[4]

---

[4]"Parenting When Apart: Tips for Non-resident Fathers" http://www.edis.ifas.ufl.edu/he139 , University of Florida, 2018.

Chapter 22:

CONFESSIONS OF A FATHER

This is a blueprint of a confession that I wrote for fathers; if you would like, you can read this to yourself, making a commitment that you will make the things written in it a priority in your life. Or you can read it with your children, or send it to them, that's if it applies to your situation. If not, you can always use it as a blueprint to write your own letter of reconciliation to them. Forgiveness will heal the deep wounds of the heart.

First aid teaches that in order to save the life of someone who's been in an accident and is bleeding, it is imperative to stop the bleeding first. Everything else is secondary. Likewise, through forgiveness and empathy, we must stop the bleeding so that all parties involved can be saved. Confession, forgiveness, and repentance is the things that can stop the bleeding.

The Confession

Son(s) or Daughter(s), I know you've tried so many things to cover or erase the hurt that I have caused you. Many of these things you have used or are using are harmful to your physical well-being. Many are harmful to your emotional, mental and spiritual well-being. But I know that you turned to those things because I wasn't there for you to turn to, and for that, I am truly sorry. I'm sorry for being the reason you've turned to these things for comfort.

I believe that if I had only been there for you, you might not have ever made most of those choices, or I could have been there to help you through the bad choices you've made. Drugs, sexual promiscuity, aggressive behavior, fighting, killing, anger, dropping out of school, etc. are some of those choices. I should have been there to show you love, protect you and give you directions.

I should have been there to help nurture your self-esteem. I should have been there when you needed a father's hug or a father's kiss. But I wasn't, and for that I am sorry. These self-destructive things may seem to get rid of the hurt, but they don't, they only mask it. I ask for your forgiveness for whatever I've done that damaged you; for not being there for you when you needed me most. Forgive me for not showing up for events like parent and teacher meetings, or not being at any of your games, dances or other activities. Forgive me for missing your birthday and for not calling you to say happy birthday.

Forgive me for the days that I spend too much time at work, or at least that's what I told you. I made money and gained success, but in the process, I lost you. And most of all, sorry for leaving you with the feeling of not being loved, by not being a priority in my life. Because you are. Please allow me to make right the wrong I've caused and the chance to make up for the time I've lost with you. Even though I can never get those times back, allow me the opportunity to make my days with you the most valuable time in my life. I may not deserve a second chance, but I ask that you would give me one, despite my unworthiness. And if you do this, I will never betray your trust and will honor this second chance.

I ask that you would let go of the anger and the disdain you have for me, even though I am deserving of it. You don't deserve the hatred that I caused to eat away at you like this. Let go of the resentment that you have towards me. Let it go, my child, because your life is too valuable for you to allow what I did to diminish your worth. I am sorry_____ (say or write their name). Forgive me for not giving you what every father should give his children: his love and attention.

Chapter 23:

TAKE WHAT THEY GIVE YOU

After reading this book, I hope that you will indeed commit to fatherhood, not out of restraint, but from a willing, forgiving and repented heart. Some fathers will make this decision when their child/children are young. Others will make this decision at its most challenging time, when their children are in their teen years. Still others will make this decision when their children are adults and have had children of their own. All these can be most challenging times, mostly for the same reason, but with the added challenge of not letting resentment from a bad relationship begin to affect the emotional, mental and spiritual well-being of the children's posterity.

The teen and adult years are when the task to rekindle a relationship with your child is most difficult, though not impossible. Nonetheless, to decide to re-enter a child's life, you must be fully committed and aware that there are consequences that come with that commitment, consequences such as the feeling not being mutual.

The teen years are when children naturally begin pulling away and when the desire for more independence increases. It is a healthy thing when children start to become more independent; this transition in life should not be stifled by parents who are afraid of losing their children to the natural phenomenon known as maturity. These are the years when they want to hang out more with their peers and less with their parents. The years when they begin to come into their own, when they think they know everything, or as the old folks used to say, "when they start smelling themselves." This is a time when they just have their own opinions. And of course, a time when they think that you know nothing because you have so matured (are too old).

It is also typically the age of rebellion and curiosity, flooded with peer pressure. You will have to deal with these natural social, emotional and mental changes as you attempt to re-establish the broken relationship between you and your child.

You must exercise being non-judgmental and empathic, showing enormous restraint in these times because they will be difficult times. These are times when you must show that you are not surprised about their actions even though their actions surprised you-; buuuut if you were ever a teenager it shouldn't surprise you. There will be times when you must not show disappointment of a child's bad decisions or actions, even though those decisions and actions may be disappointing.

It is my experience that displaying disappointment, displeasure or frustration about the actions of a child is not always a good thing. Often when a parent shows disappointment, annoyance or frustration about something their child did, it makes that child afraid to confide in that parent for fear of being judged. By always showing displeasure towards something they've done, it makes them shut down totally, and any constructive conversation a parent could have had is lost. Even though a parent may have every right to be disappointed, displeased or frustrated, it still doesn't make it the right time to show those emotions. Sometimes what we've done as fathers forfeits our right to show any displeasure for our children's activities, but it should force us to use the much greater tool of empathy—which will make way for the teachable moments. If you're genuinely committed to the pursuit of fatherhood, there are times you must embrace, not the acts but those who commit the acts.

Just because you've repented and are now ready to be the kind of father that you should have been doesn't mean that your child is prepared to accept you. You must understand that you have hurt this child. Most likely, they may have witnessed the tremendous hardships their mother has had to go through because of your absence. Yes, your lack of involvement in your child's life can harm the mother mentally and emotionally.

Many times, children have watched their mothers struggle not only to take on their motherly obligations, but also trying to fulfil the responsibility on which you defaulted. They've watched their mother work overtime to give them the bare necessities of life, while still giving them the attention they needed, even if it meant neglecting her needs and health.

Mothers are often overly stressed because of the absence of co-parenting skills of a father. Some children witness their mothers crying under the burden of this tremendous task. Because of this, they will want nothing to do with you and could care less about your change of heart. But even though such disdain exists, you must be patient and relentless in your pursuit of reconnecting.

It would be best if you remained diligent, even in the presence of their rejection. A child's rejection of you does not release you from your obligation as a father. Again, this is a difficult task, and it requires patience, understanding and diligence on your part, but none the less a doable task. You must also be willing to accept that child for who they are and what they've become. Your goal must be to forge and create a better relationship with your child. It would be best if you remembered that you had something to do with how this child feels and behaves.

To make a change in someone, you must first build a relationship with that person. When you work on changing the relationship rather than trying to change the child, you will begin to see positive results. You must also be willing to work within the parameters your child will give you, and not try to impose your will on them. However wide they chose to open the door of acceptance; you must accept it and work within whatever opening they decide to give.

If they crack the door a little bit, don't try to force your way in because you want to get inside. Instead, slip whatever you can through that crack of opportunity. If they chose to communicate with you through a closed door, then talk to them through that closed door. At least, there is some communication; the closed door is irrelevant, but communication is the beginning of a better relationship.

Always remember that a collapsed wall began with a small crack. Most children want their fathers in their life, but because of what that father may have done or didn't do, that child will be reluctant to put themselves out there to be possibly hurt again by that father. You must show that you're worthy of their acceptance and that you won't hurt them to that extent ever again. They need to see how badly you want them; they need to know by your actions how important they are to you; because as far as they're concerned, you've already shown them how bad you didn't want them.

Are you willing to work through the rejection and the contempt they have for you, however long or hard they make it for you to do so? Or will you stop trying? Will you give up your pursuit of fatherhood and abandon them again because of these difficulties? Welcome to the quest of fatherhood! Take it or leave it. You've already done the latter.

Chapter 24:

THE P.R.I.D.E. OF FATHERHOOD

All fathers have pride. Here is my acronym for **P.R.I.D.E.** as it relates to fatherhood pride.

P- PRESENT- A father must be consistently there for his children. His presence must be physically and visually evident in his children's lives.

R -RESPONSIBLE- A father should make the rearing of his children his number one responsibility. The father should be the example of what responsible men do. He must take responsibility for the things that his children see and hear while in his presence.

Our children should not see everything that can be seen. Our children should not hear everything that can be heard. Our children should not touch everything that can be touched. Everything that can be said should not be said, especially around our children. There is a time and a place for all things to happen.

A father must be wise and responsible enough to know the time and place to have specific conversations and to do and hear certain things. When a parent says something like:

"They're going to see it regardless" or "They're going to do it when I'm not around, so they might as will do it here in my house", that parent has given up their responsibility as a role model and teacher, essentially relinquishing their ability to set rules. That parent is conceding to irresponsibility, reckless living and thoughtlessness because it is easier to do that than to parent responsibly. So, they become irresponsible parents raising irresponsible children in the comfort of their own homes. This is irresponsibility at its best. My mom said to me before, "When you get your own house, then you can do whatever you want in your house. But since this is my house, you do as I say."

I- INVOLVEMENT: This is the entire basis of this book: fathers being actively involved in the lives of their children. Even though this book is about fathers, both parents must be included in their children's lives. Both parents must have a positive influence on their children's educational, social, mental, emotional and spiritual well-being. Especially if you have younger children, don't be so adult-oriented that you can't do childish things with them. Doing childish things with them creates lasting memories; it makes them comfortable with you and they become able to relate to you more. They will feel that what is important to them is important to you as well. So, learn to be foolish, silly and child-like.

D- DEVOTED: To be devoted is to have a great dedication and loyalty to something or someone. Our children must know and feel that they have our utmost devotion. Fathers must give themselves over to the display, discipline and study of fatherhood.

E- EMOTION: Fathers, it is important that our children see us as humans and not as the enigmatic figure they know as "I'M YOUR FATHER." They must be able to see the human factor. They need to see when we're disappointed, hurt and angry. More importantly, they need to see the positive ways we handle our emotions when facing difficult times. They must know that the display of emotions like anger, disappointment and hurt are all human emotions and that it's OK to be human.

Sometimes it is not good to hide our weakest moments from our kids. Because in hiding our weaknesses from them, we hide from them what it takes to overcome weakness. They must be made to feel comfortable and confident that your love will remain steadfast, constant and unconditional, despite the display of their weakness and of being human. They care little about the mistakes you make along the way; you are still their father, and they would hope that you would feel the same way about them. Loosen up Daddy; be human and it will open doors that you otherwise would have never opened. This is the P.R.I.D.E. of fatherhood.

Chapter 25:
THE PURSUIT OF FATHERHOOD

Fathers come in all sizes, colors, religions, faiths and beliefs. They have different political persuasions and come from different social and economic backgrounds. None of these factors have any bearing on what it takes to be a father. None of these things, whether or not you agree with them, disqualifies a man from being a father. It is our involvement with our children that makes us better fathers and mothers. If we as fathers abandon our children, we abandon ourselves. If we ignore them, we ignore our manhood. Once we have been part of the process of bringing a child into this world, we become one part of the highest calling in the universe, fatherhood, with the other highest calling being motherhood.

Our kids are our most precious possession, and we must treat them as such. We are and forever will be their "daddy." Although there are some great substitutes out there, none is as good as the biological father. None is as powerful and as influential as the one who they call *Daddy*. None is as inherently compatible with nurturing, as the man whose genes forever runs through that child's being. The presence of a father is irreplaceable. It is a match made in heaven, and a life lived on earth.

If we abandon our duties as fathers, we forfeit our successes, and we delay our development as a man. If we step away from fatherhood, we step out of manhood; we deny ourselves from becoming blessed among men.

When active fathers give their children the faith to believe in their dreams and the strength to bring those dreams to fruition, fathers help instill in their daughters the self-esteem and self-respect they need as women. Your daughters will not settle for less than what they see in you. They will not need a man to validate who they are because you, their father, has installed that validation in them. They will look for a man who will compliment who they are.

As for your sons, you instill in them what it truly means to be a man, that a true man doesn't run away from his responsibilities; they run to it. You are the wind beneath their wings. You are the sail that catches their inspiration and propels them ahead through the sea of life. When the chips are down, they need only to look up and see you assuring them that all is not lost. You are one of a kind, indispensable and irreplaceable. Your weaknesses become their strength because they've watched you persevere through adversities. Your defeats and victories are the compasses that direct them; your success gives hope to them. Your failures become lessons in life.

Your voice is unmistakably comforting to them; your presence floods their souls with unspeakable joy. Your touch comforts and assures them that you will not abandon them, because you are them, and they are you. You are their daddy, and yet with all your imperfections and human mistakes, to them, you're the closest thing to God.

I wish you well in your pursuit of fatherhood.

Chapter 26:

WORDS FROM THE FATHERS

TESTIMONIES FROM NON-RESIDENTIAL FATHERS

In this section of the book, you will read some testimonies of great fathers who, like me, are not perfect, but despite their imperfections pursued fatherhood. Non-residential fathers around the country are dealing with similar issues every day. You are not alone in the struggle. I thought that perhaps having other non-residential fathers share their experiences and advice would help you in your pursuit of fatherhood. In these testimonies of great fathers, I share them with you just as they have written them. Enjoy!

Testimony #1:

Being a non-residential father has had a profound impact on my life. I often look back and think if I could have done anything differently. I considered going back to the relationship to "make it work for the kids," but once I came to my senses, I realized I would only be giving them false hope. Sometimes we think staying in a relationship or returning to a failed relationship is the best thing for the children when, in reality, it does more damage than good. Kids are a lot smarter than we think. Sometimes they can realize that the relationship is over before the adults do. I truly believe children who grow up in a household where the parents are just "hanging in there for the kids" are more than likely to do the same once they marry, especially men. Those marriages usually have trust issues and end in divorce. Society has told us that we aren't responsible if we leave our families, but I disagree. I can't make anyone happy if I'm not happy and neither can you.

I grew up without a father in the house, so I was not aware that there is a difference between a father's relationship with his children and his relationship with the mother of his children. I thought getting married was the cure for a generational curse of repeating the cycle of fathers/stepfathers and mothers/stepmothers. My relationship with my father is what caused me to think that way. I was literally trying to correct the (perceived) wrongs of my father's life and the way he handled his fatherly duties. I once heard someone refer to it as "fighting my daddy's devil." It's a powerful and eye-opening experience when you realize you're fighting a battle you'd lost before the fight began. That led to some of my early failures as a non-residential father.

I used to think it was OK if I just saw my children every other weekend. After all, that's what my father did. But I vividly remember being dropped off at home after an exciting weekend with my father and missing him the second I saw his car pull off. I didn't want that for my children. Besides, I miss them just as much as they miss me. So, I would, and do still to this day, pick them up WHENEVER I can.

There's no substitution for a father being in his son's life. There's no better feeling than having your daughter look at you as if you walk on water. The opportunity to shape, mold and influence their lives is PRICELESS. I do admit, it has cost me quite a few relationships. I've had women tell me I couldn't provide the time it took to build a relationship with them because I spent too much time with my kids. As a non-residential father, that was confirmation that I was doing the right thing. It was also, confirmation that I was dating the wrong woman. If a woman can't recognize, understand and appreciate your commitment as a father, she doesn't need to be in your life.

I would give this advice to all non-residential fathers, ESPECIALLY those who are African American and between the ages of 18-25. The foundation and example you set now—RIGHT NOW—will determine the future of your children's children. Your son will raise his children according to the way he was raised. Your daughter will attract men with the character that you possess. If that's not enough to challenge you to be the best father you can be, I don't know what will. Ask yourself, did the mother of your child/children have a good relationship with the father figure in her life? It's an important question when you think about it because some women, especially those who are bitter and spiteful towards you are that way because of a lack of respect for a man that was or wasn't in her life. It has nothing to do with you. You are just the punching bag for her upon which to release her frustration. But we as men and now as fathers have to do a better job choosing the women we deal with and more importantly, have children with. When we do that, EVERYONE benefits, especially the children.

Peace and blessings,

~Mod

Testimony #2:

I grew up on the rough streets of Newark, New Jersey, where there was no time for love, only survival. Being the youngest of four, a mother's love was the only love given at that moment. My dad, who was a wonderful man in his short life, loved me. But he did not teach or show me the way to love.

As a teenager, things became different for me. I became a womanizer and obtained a cold heart towards females. When I finally reached manhood, one day I received a phone call stating that I was no longer alone. It was at that moment that I was introduced to fatherhood. As a father, life became very difficult. I was not around my daughter or her mother a lot. When I did show up, I thought money was the key to being a father. I would come over with all types of gifts, from toys to coats. You name it; I purchased it. Then one day changed my life completely.

One day I picked up my daughter and took her to my apartment; I had tons of toys for her once again. But this time, gifts were not enough. Within 15 minutes, she became very upset and started to cry. I asked her what was wrong, and she said, "I don't know you; leave me alone and take me back to my mommy." That statement alone knocked me to my knees. My eyes filled with tears, and that's when I realized as a father, I could not buy love. From that day on, me and my daughter's relationship has been wonderful. We do any and everything together. I can't get enough of spending time with her. She is a teenager now, and somehow money has come back into play with things like hair, nails, clothes and other teenage things. But I still keep my promise of loving her.

~Sam

Testimony #3:

I have been a non-residential father for just one year, but I miss my children so much that I feel like I am dying from loneliness. I am constantly arguing with my ex about keeping my children too long. I only get to spend time with them every other weekend. Whenever they come over, the kids always want to go out or away, but I just want to spend time with them at home doing regular things because they are not always with me. I miss my children so much that I have found myself saying that I would get back with my ex-wife just so I could spend more time with my kids. I find myself constantly trying to convince my children that my separating from their mother did not have anything to do with them and that it was not their fault.

~ Emmitt

Testimony #4

Hi, my name is Butch, and I am a non-residential father of my three kids. I have only had visitation rights for the last ten years. The mother of my children and I have been on and off for about seven years and have not been together for the last three years. I think separation and divorce are good if the parties cannot get along, but I believe it is hard on children even though they eventually learn to adapt. I have seen my kids crying, upset and out of control for the last three years, coming and going to and from visitation. One of my biggest issues is when court rulings and mutual agreements are declared or implied, and there is no one to see that it is correctly carried out. The law is often carried out by a letter, not the spirit.

I love my children and every free moment I have; I try to spend with them. But it is aggravating when you have to visit your kids based on a system. Going fishing, to the park and to the movies are all nice, but the one thing I most regret is that I cannot share in their experience on a daily basis. The pain I see them go through when they are not with me or when I have to leave and say goodbye, sometimes makes me wish in my heart that I'd never had them.

One challenge in raising my children is when my ex-wife and I filed for divorce. I agreed to her keeping the house and the children. I am responsible for sending child support monthly, and the money is supposed to be used to take care of my children, but every time I talk to them, they are in dire need of things. When I go to pick them up, I cannot go into my own home because of the legal system. Me knowing that I am spending my hard-earned money to take care of my ex-wife and her boyfriend and cannot enter the home which I own and pay for monthly, frustrates me tremendously.

When I go to the house to pick up my kids, my ex-wife's boyfriend answers the door and tells me to wait a minute and then sends the children out to me. He doesn't even let me in knowing that I own the house. These are some of the things that aggravate me and other non-residential fathers like me. It is not as easy as people may believe for non-residential fathers who try to take care of and be responsible for their children.

~Butch

Testimony #5

All praises due to Allah for allowing me to write this so that it might help the many souls it reaches. I am a father of 10, and Allah has blessed me to be in their lives. But I find the system makes it very difficult to be a father because they want to tell you how to raise your children.

There are certain things that I miss about being with my children. I do not have the opportunity to teach them self-respect, how to dress as women, and how to be young men. I find it difficult to understand how the law can require my money to take care of my children, but not allow me to raise them in my own way. I love my children, but part of love is showing them the right things to do. It becomes very frustrating when I show them one way, and their mother shows them something contrary. One of the major things I miss is not being able to teach my children discipline.

May Allah Bless You,

~Mujahid

Testimony #6

Hello, my name is Kevin. I am not an American; I am Haitian. I have been in America for eight years and have not seen my family in three years. I am in the act of trying to bring my family here to America. It is so very painful for me, with a

161

loving wife and four boys, not to have them here with me. America has been wonderful, but I have been using every dime I have to try to get them here with me. The last time I saw them, my son Samuel was at my wife's waist. Now he is taller than her. I have not been able to see them grow.

I talk to them twice per week and I'm always crying on the phone while I talk to them, but they don't know it. I send them money every month. My wife and I pray every day that they can get here quickly. I am a general contractor by profession and have done well for myself, but possessions cannot replace having my family with me. I often wonder if it was really worth it to come to America. My wife sends me pictures, but I can only imagine what it would be like to be there with them.

Peace,

~Kevin

Testimony #7

Hello, my name is Joseph. I am writing this letter to help other fathers and to relieve myself. I am the product of a broken family and as such, I swore that I would not have children and not be with them. So, for the last five years, I have agonized about not being with my children. One, because I miss them and two, because I don't believe children ever get over it.

I have two boys, Jeff and Mitchell. Through the grace of God, they are doing fantastic in school. One is in the 7th grade, and the other is in the 9th grade. One plays football and the other plays soccer. Because I cannot spend a lot of time with them due to legal issues, they tend to gravitate towards their stepfather. I find myself constantly angry because of the relationship they are developing with him. I feel it should be mine. I do not have the opportunity to be in their lives on a daily basis to see them grow, but someone else shares in everything I dream about.

My children do not understand why I cannot be with them every day. My job requires a lot of hands-on interaction and unfortunately, it is a global position, so I am not able to be home as much as I would like. I took to drinking to help smother the pain of not having them in my life. Since I cannot be with them as much as I would like, I give them lots of gifts as a substitute for my presence. Their mother tells me all the time that I give them too much, and I'm spoiling them. But when I ask for more time, she tells me no. This is just something else I have been battling for the last five years.

I love them more than myself. I wish that I could support them at every soccer and football game; tell them and show them all the time how much I love them. But it often feels impossible due to personal attacks from their mother and stepfather. ~Joseph

Testimony #8

My major experiences as a non-residential father has been the many times my kids did not understand when I have to leave them after a visit. I'm a father of three children: two girls and a boy. It is particularly challenging when the weekends they spend with me come to an end, especially for my daughters. It has been reported by their mom and their teachers that their behavior changes immediately after spending a week with me. People do not understand that I go through as much pain as they do when my children have to leave me.

Another challenge is the many questions I get from my children like: "What happened?" "Why aren't you and mom together?" and "Are you going to get back together?". It is very difficult for me not to have an answer for my children. My son Kilard said that he prays that we will get back together and be a family again. It hurts me so much because I know that his mother and I will not be together again. It is equally bothersome when I go into their room and see their clothes, toys and games. Pictures of our times together having fun, hanging out, joking and sharing, flash into my mind. I also have flashes of them while doing daily work and talking to people, especially when I see other dads with their children. This is just a little of what I experience. It would take a lifetime for me to tell everything. Thanks for your listening ear.

God bless you, ~ Michael

Testimony #9

Hi, my name is Daddy, but you can call me Dad or Father if you'd like. It is my job to take care of you; to make sure you always feel loved and safe. It's my duty to make sure you always have food in your stomach, clothes on your back and a roof over your head. I will do my best to not only teach you about doing what's morally and ethically right, but to lead by example. I might be a little rough on you when it comes to things like education, self-respect and being responsible, but that's a part of loving you. I know how important education is, and because I love you so much, I will risk you being mad at me so that I can assure you get a quality education and lead a successful life.

There will come the day when I chase boys away. That falls under my duty of keeping you safe. Not only will I ensure that no one hurts you physically, but emotionally as well. I will teach you how a real man treats a woman so you won't waste your time. And if one should happen to be slick enough to slip through the cracks, I will be there to comfort you and make you feel better.

You are my princess and one day you will be someone's queen. Anyone not willing to treat you as such needs to keep it moving. It may not always seem like it, but I will always be your best friend and biggest supporter. You can talk to me about anything. I want to be the first person you come to when you need anything, whether it's a shoulder to cry on or an ear to listen to you. My love for you far outweighs my love for anything or anyone in the world! You are the greatest thing that has ever and will ever happen to me! I love you dearly!

~Jermaine Brown

Chapter 27:

WHO'S YOUR DADDY'S
Information and Education Centre

This section of the book is where non-residential fathers, as well as residential fathers, can find inspiration, information, and education through any one of these listed organizations and people. We all can use some help in our efforts to become better fathers. So, I've researched some groups and websites and posted them in the book so that even after you've finished reading the book, you can have some information to go to for yourself or you can refer it to someone else. I hope the sources are useful in your effort and your pursuit towards fatherhood as a non-residential and residential father.

FATHERHOOD

Website: www.pursuitoffatherhood.wix.com/fatherhood
This is my blog; check it out!

DADDY UNIVERSITY

Website: www.daddyuniv.com

As the oldest Male Parenting Education Company, we educate, advocate and support men raising children. Here you will find information to help you through the tough times, confusing times and the greatest times of your life. The President/CEO of Daddy University, Inc. uses the hard-won tips, tricks and skills that he picked up as a father of four in order to guide and inspire other dads in need of a helping hand.

NATIONAL CENTER FOR FATHERING

Website: www.fathers.com

The National Center for Fathering (NCF) was founded as a non-profit in 1990, with the purpose of "turning the hearts of fathers to their children." In the late 1980s, Ken Canfield conducted research on fathering while pursuing his Ph.D. After studying the existing statistics and research, he arrived at the undeniable conclusion that helping men become better fathers is perhaps the most strategic way to benefit children and strengthen families. It was through this conclusion that NCF was born.

NATIONAL FATHERHOOD INITIATIVE

Website: www.fatherhood.org

National Fatherhood Initiative® is a 501(c)3 non-profit organization founded in 1994 to reverse our nation's destructive trend towards the father's absence. Therefore, NFI's mission is to improve the well-being of children by increasing the proportion of children with involved, responsible and committed fathers in their lives.

NATIONAL RESPONSIBLE FATHERHOOD CLEARINGHOUSE

Website: www.fatherhood.gov

The National Responsible Fatherhood Clearinghouse is an Office of Family Assistance (OFA) funded national resource for fathers, practitioners, programs/federal grantees, states and the public at-large who are serving or interested in supporting strong fathers and families.

SKIP

Website: www.skipinc.org
SKIP, Inc. Community Resource Services was founded by Mrs. Gloria Jean Canty-Williams in 1976.

SKIP's mission is to provide support services to children of incarcerated parents and their families and to increase public awareness of the underlying problems of these children as victims through education, advocacy and research. The purpose of SKIP programs is to help children ("Skippers") of incarcerated parents and their families better cope with separation due to incarceration, to maintain family ties and to break the cycle of incarceration.

INSTITUTE OF DEVELOPMENT FOR AFRICAN AMERICAN YOUTH

Website: www.idaay.org

The Institute for the Development of African-American Youth, Inc. (IDAAY) was founded by S. Archye Leacock and a colleague in May 1991. This organization has been formed in response to the alarming statistics characterizing the high level of violence reflected in the lives of disadvantaged youth in the Philadelphia area.

FATHERS AND FAMILY CENTER

Website: www.fathersandfamiliescenter.org

Fathers and Families Center exists to break a dysfunctional cycle and to replace it with something new—a cycle that dismisses the notion of poverty and absentee fatherhood as inevitable. This new cycle brings hope for the future, and rewards hard work, education and engagement. Most importantly, it honors the commitment it takes to be a great father and a great man who understands his responsibilities to his kids.

FIT DADDY 365

Website: www.fitdaddy365.com

Fit Daddy 365 is the brainchild of Soren Harrison. Its mission is to motivate, inspire, and teach us to be fitter, better dads, both physically and mentally, and emotionally through the use of online training and courses built just for dads by a dad.

Ray Mingo

S p e a k e r
pursuitoffatherhood@yahoo.com

"Wishing you well in your pursuit of fatherhood."

www.ingramcontent.com/pod-product-compliance
Lightning Source LLC
Chambersburg PA
CBHW031300090426
42742CB00007B/536